AN

ESSAY

ON THE

PHILOSOPHICAL EVIDENCE

OF

CHRISTIANITY;

ETC.

G. WOODFALL, ANGEL COURT, SKINNER STREET, LONDON.

AN ESSAY

ON THE

PHILOSOPHICAL EVIDENCE

OF

CHRISTIANITY;

OR,

THE CREDIBILITY OBTAINED

TO A

SCRIPTURAL REVELATION,

FROM ITS COINCIDENCE WITH THE FACTS OF NATURE.

BY THE REVEREND

RENN D. HAMPDEN, M.A.

LATE FELLOW OF ORIEL COLLEGE, OXFORD.

—— what if earth
Be but the shadow of Heaven, and things therein
Each to other like, more than on earth is thought?
PARADISE LOST, v. 574.

LONDON:

JOHN MURRAY, ALBEMARLE STREET.

MDCCCXXVII.

PREFACE.

ADMIRATION of the celebrated treatise of Bishop Butler,—" The Analogy of Religion, Natural and Revealed, to the Constitution and Course of Nature",—and a desire to obtain a full comprehension of the character and force of the particular evidence exemplified in that work, have been the primary inducements to the following attempt to elucidate the principle on which that evidence proceeds, and the importance of its application to such a religion as Christianity.

A discussion of this kind appeared the more necessary, as the evidence of the natural world has been greatly underrated in the general estimate, as a constituent of the great Christian Argument. It is usual to speak of it, indiscriminately, under the general head of the internal evidence, and, accordingly, to contrast it with the external evidence derived from facts belonging to the history of Christianity.—Now, though it may rightly be classed under the head of the internal evidence, inasmuch as it respects the internal system and character of the religion itself contained in any revelation; yet is it also an evidence from external facts, inasmuch as it is conversant about the phenomena of nature. And it ought not, therefore, to be *contrasted* with the evidence usually termed external, as if it offered a proof of a different kind; but to be *distinguished* from it simply in respect of, the subject-matter of its facts, and the points of the revelation to which it applies those facts. The facts which the evidence, properly external, employs, are the events which have accompanied the promulgation and establishment of the religion in question. The facts which that kind of internal evidence here examined employs, are those which are collected from observation of the established course of Divine Providence in the world.—The former applies the test of facts to a given religion, considered as an *historical* event. The latter applies the test of facts to a given religion, considered, in its *structure* as a system of truths, and in the *nature* of its evidences and circumstances in general,—the *nature* of its evidences and circumstances clearly presenting a point of comparison distinct from their application as *actual events*. It applies, for instance, to Christianity, either as containing the doctrine of the atonement; or as miraculous in its essential evidence,— as deficient in its proof,—not universal in its diffusion, &c.

From not distinctly considering then, that there is an internal evidence conversant about facts (and not mere opinions) no less than the external,—the argument of " The Analogy " has been involved in that suspicion, which justly attaches to all speculations à priori on the subject of religion, or attempts to ascertain the intrinsic merits of a given revelation, by its accordance with preconceived notions unsupported by adequate data: instead of its being regarded in its true light, as a deduction, in the first place, of principles of theological truth from actual observations; and then, an application of the principles so deduced to the doctrinal and circumstantial nature of the religion,—and consequently an argument à posteriori in its principle, though in the mode of its application it assumes the form of à priori reasoning.

Nor can it be reasonably objected, that this *form* of the argument renders this Evidence obnoxious to the charge of a vain speculation: since, not even our application of the external evidence is exempt from the like imperfection. For, whilst in arguing the historical truth of Christianity we commence with the fact of its present existence, and those other facts which the testimonies of historians have transmitted to us, relative to its existence antecedently to our own times,—yet, that we may apply these facts as proofs of the divinity of its origin, we must consider, whether they are such as may be conceived to have been the result of a supposed divine origin. We must put ourselves in the imaginary situation of persons who are not in possession of the effect produced; and argue what would be the effect, on the supposition that the alleged revelation were really from God, in the events belonging to it. And thus, our inquiry is satisfied on finding the concluded event coincident with the real and known effect. As, for instance,—the rapid propagation of the gospel at its outset, is a known fact in its history;—but, before we can apply this fact to the proof of its divine origin, we speculate concerning the probable effect in a case where the hand of God is supposed to be immediately exerted; and the conclusion from such an assumption is, that the truth so supported would be rapidly propagated, in spite of all opposition from the world;—agreeably to the known fact.

There being, accordingly, a means of substantiating by facts the internal economy of revealed truth, it follows, that there is an intimate and proper philosophy of religion; and not merely an external philosophy, or application of the general laws of evidence to the particular evidence adduced in favour of any religion,—as is implied in those statements which rest the credibility of a religion solely and exclusively on the testimonies to its existence as an *historical* event.

At the same time, it will readily be acknowledged, there is a strong prima facie objection to the assertion of a philosophical theology. We appear, in holding such language, to be exceeding our proper limits, as the simple recipients of a gracious illumination from the Divine wisdom; and to be presumptuously reducing into system and order, where we ought rather to be devoutly ascribing, not only our measure of divine knowledge in general, but every particular matter revealed, both in its substance and method, to the good pleasure of God. We seem to be theorising, when we ought to be obeying,—to be giving to knowledge the prerogatives of faith and love.—The objection, it is trusted, will be found to apply rather to the name of philosophy, than to its right use in the study of religion. So far as the argument pursued in "The Analogy" is valid, there is a sound philosophy of religion; and it is only to that extent, and in that sense, that the assertion of it is here advanced.

Nor is it only in respect of its essential nature, that the Evidence here investigated has been underrated; but its importance has been limited to the purpose of invalidating objections against Christianity,—its positive subserviency, as an argument to the truth of the religion, being regarded as comparatively little. This disesteem of the Evidence is a result of that mistaken view of its nature already adverted to. For if it be considered merely as an argument à priori, it may still be triumphantly employed against an adversary, who brings objections against the religion drawn from speculations of a similar kind; but no real evidence can be obtained from it of the internal truth of the religion to which it may be applied; since it then has no foundation in nature. It is then only an argumentum ad hominem. This limitation, however, of the service of the Evidence, whether it proceed from a wrong estimate of its nature, or not, is certainly very common among even professed admirers of " The Analogy". Probably it has arisen, in some degree, from the method pursued by Bishop Butler himself, in directing the attention of the reader, throughout the work, to the force with which the Evidence repels speculative objections. To remove this misapprehension, as well as the former, a full investigation of the merits of the Evidence appeared to be demanded; that the various ways, in which it administers to the cause of the Christian Revelation, might distinctly be placed before the view.

An additional motive to this inquiry suggested itself in a conviction of the injustice of that prejudice, with which the admirable work of Bishop Butler is regarded by some, as a work full of intricacy and obscurity. If there be no ground for accusing a writer of confusion of thought, the apparent obscurity of his writings may, in that case, be ascribed to a want, in the reader, of a previous due acquaintance with the subject of which they treat. Now, all ground of the former charge must be entirely removed when we apply our criticism to such a writer as Butler; and it may, therefore, be concluded, that a preliminary consideration of the nature and grounds of the argument pursued in the work is what is required, for some readers, to dissipate that appearance of obscurity with which it is overcast. The student, indeed, who has not conceived just notions of the nature of the Evidence, is not immediately aware, as he reads, that the right prosecution of the argument essentially precludes all theories concerning the subjects discussed, and, consequently, all modes of expression, as far as is possible, which involve particular theories in them. To avoid the fallacy, which the introduction of such theories in his language would occasion, Butler is often obliged to employ a circuitous, and apparently awkward, style in stating his arguments; or, as he says himself, in reference to the principles of liberty and moral fitness, has "sometimes been obliged to express himself in a manner which will appear strange to such as do not observe the reason for it"*. Thus, in his chapter on a Future Life, he does not speak of the soul, as an immaterial, or naturally immortal, principle; since his object is, to employ such arguments as would be conclusive, whatever theory of the soul be maintained; appealing, simply, to such facts as are signs of its posthumous existence, whatever may be its nature. Hence his use of such expressions as "faculties of perception and action"—"living powers"—"living agents"—"the

* Butler's Works, by Halifax, Vol. I. p. 398, Oxford Ed. 1820.

living being each man calls himself"—&c.: which, to be justly estimated, must be regarded as exclusions of any particular theory concerning the soul; so as to leave the question of a future life, as there entered into, purely a question of fact. And so throughout the treatise, it will be found, on a close examination, that it is the difficulty of stating an accurate generalization of particular facts, exempt from all particular theories of the subjects about which they are conversant, which occasions a difficulty in the style. Had a more familiar expression been employed, though founded on some abstruse speculation, the apparent difficulty would have been less, whilst a real perplexity would have been introduced into the argument, from the fallacy involved in the more specious term. Conclusions of the kind employed in "The Analogy" differ from mere speculative conclusions, in being drawn immediately and wholly from the facts examined. In stating them, therefore, we cannot proceed a step beyond the limits of the facts. Great precision of language, accordingly, is required, in order to exhibit them faithfully. And they exact from the reader the like patient and close attention, in order that he may perceive their true outline, and know why such a particular form of expression is used in each instance, and not one more usual and obvious.

At the same time, it is not meant, by what is here said, to defend every particular expression employed in the conduct of the argument of " The Analogy ", as the most appropriate and simple;—or to assert, that other forms might not sometimes have been substituted, at once accurate, and more familiar to the general reader,—or, that greater expansion of the reasoning, with less of that allusion to collateral topics of discussion, with which, the very comprehensiveness of his mind, and his forecast of possible objections to particular statements, have led him occasionally to interrupt the straightforward course of his argument—would not have given greater perspicuity to it, without diminishing its force. It is only meant to remove that general imputation of obscurity, which is carelessly and unjustly cast upon the work. That there is some degree of obscurity arising from the nature of the discussion pursued in " The Analogy," it must be conceded; and it is to the removal of this, that the inquiry here instituted into the grounds, nature, and importance, of the Evidence itself illustrated in that work, is intended to serve.

The separate arrangement, adopted by Butler, of the arguments from the constitution and course of nature, as they refer to natural or revealed religion, has not been followed in this Essay; because, when once it is admitted, that religion has been authenticated and enlarged by a distinct communication from God, it seems, that nature is then superseded, as *the source* of instruction on the subject, by the more express and copious subsequent information: and we have only to examine how far nature leads us on the same track of divine truth, and confirms and illustrates the words of her successor: ranging the scriptures exclusively on one side, as containing the truths of religion, and the instruction of nature on the other, as containing their evidence. Butler's arrangement, however, is not objectionable in itself; since the concession of some fundamental truths to the province of natural religion, by no means implies, that such truths were originally discovered, or are necessarily discoverable, by dint of human reason. Natural and revealed religion may be contradistinguished, in respect of the truths properly belonging to each; the former containing those truths which result from our relations to God, as the Lord of the visible world; the latter containing those truths which result from our relations to God, as the Lord of the invisible world. Now, in the case of those belonging to the latter class, their origin must be known to us, because we have no other means of apprehending them, but by supernatural revelation. In the case of those belonging to the former class, as they exist in nature, they may be traced in nature, whether originally obtained in the same way, or otherwise.

If we suppose nature to have been intended as an independent organ of divine communication; yet it may consistently be supposed, that a miraculous *unfolding* of the truths contained in nature, may have been necessary *in the first instance* to open the mind of man to a perception of those truths;—in like manner, as immediate oral instruction from the ministers of scripture truths appears to have been a necessary accompaniment of the word of God, in order to *introduce* the knowledge supernaturally revealed to the understanding of the future reader of scripture. " For natural religion", as Bishop Butler remarks, " may be externally revealed by God, as the ignorant may be taught it by mankind, their fellow-creatures."* And it is, moreover, " to be

* Anal. Part II. ch. vii. p. 358.

remembered," according to another observation of this excellent author, " that how much soever the establishment of natural religion in the world, is owing to the scripture-revelation, this does not destroy the proof of religion from reason, any more than the proof of Euclid's Elements is destroyed, by a man's knowing or thinking, that he should never have seen the truth of the several propositions contained in it, nor had those propositions come into his thoughts, but for that mathematician."*

It requires certainly great caution, in the separate consideration of the two classes of theological truth, lest we transfer to the head of natural religion what belongs to the scriptures alone, and thus disparage the work of the Holy Spirit manifested in the oracles of inspiration. Perhaps the titles of some of the chapters in the first part of " The Analogy ", as expressing more than is justly due to the revelation of nature, may lead to the supposition, that the

* Id. p. 367.

whole theological truth, as nakedly stated in them, is attributed to natural religion. But it is from the discussion of the different points indicated by these titles, that we must take our estimate of the extent of natural religion, so far as it is conceived to be intimated to us by the signs of nature: and there we find its pretensions stated with due moderation and reserve.

As the scriptures are here considered as the storehouse of theological truths; so also the division of the system of nature into natural and moral, has been disregarded in reference to the present subject. Both natural and moral truths are considered here, indiscriminately, as parts of the great system of nature. Though, in another point of view, indeed, the natural system of the world is but a subordinate part of the moral, or the intellectual (as it is termed in the phraseology of Cudworth); since every thing in the world is evidently intended to be the means of moral and intellectual improvement to a creature made capable of perceiving in it this use. If we were inquiring, accordingly, into the moral evidence of the scripture-revelation, then it would be necessary to look at nature only as it presents a moral aspect,—collecting its facts, not simply as real existences, but as containing indications of right and wrong. But our object in this inquiry being, to observe in general WHATEVER IS, in that portion of God's creation which He has submitted to the ken of our present faculties, we are no further concerned with the moral qualities of the facts observed, than as they fall under the head of actual phenomena in the course and constitution of the world. And, consequently, in this point of view, the moral system of the universe is subordinate to the natural.

AN ESSAY

ON THE

PHILOSOPHICAL EVIDENCE

OF

CHRISTIANITY.

ARGUMENT.

The necessity of examining into the character of any assumed revelation, arises from the intervention of human instruments in its delivery. Two modes of prosecuting the examination. 1st. By à priori reasoning from the principles of our nature. 2d. By comparison with the works of creation. The latter the subject of the present inquiry. Heads of inquiry :—1. The grounds of the credibility derived to a revelation from such a comparison. 2. The nature of it. 3. Its importance. 4. The consideration of objections to the employment of such an evidence.

I. The grounds of the credibility. The comparison implies, that the natural world is a kind of revelation,—that it is so, argued from the adjustment of our minds to the condition in which we are placed;—the question concerning the grounds of credibility then turns upon the existence of some common principles in the two systems of divine instruction—our repugnance to admit a scriptural revelation, on account of its improbability, raises a presumption, that there are such internal tests of its probability—a presumption also arises from the analogy of our knowledge in general—but contrary presumptions from the form and character of a scriptural revelation.—It is certain, that the two kinds of divine instruction cannot disagree—1. from both being the works of the same Divine Author—2. from both being addressed to the same human nature.—The credibility into which we are inquiring, requires some positive agreement, and not the mere absence of disagreement. Intimations of such positive agreement in passages of scripture. The proof of the existence of some common principles in the systems of nature and the scriptures, not to be confounded with the power of applying them with confidence from one class of facts to the other—the proof of the existence of some common principles, depends on the *nature* of the information which an inspired messenger may impart.— All our knowledge of God obtained from experience is *relative*—and we are incapable of attaining to a higher kind of knowledge, even from express revelation, as appears—1. from the fixed standard of our faculties—2. from the employment of human ideas in the revelation— 3. from the employment of language.—Hence it follows, that there must be some common principles in the two systems of instruction.—What those principles are, inferred from the practical character which must belong to any true revelation.—No religious knowledge can be merely speculative.—A revelation, in order to be both true and practical, must supply such motives of action, as may readily combine with those ordinary principles of conduct which we obtain from the course of nature. This requires that the two systems should unfold the same general laws of the divine procedure—which laws of the divine procedure are the media of comparison, or grounds on which the internal credibility of the scriptures is rested.

II. The nature of that credibility.—Preliminary consideration of the extent to which natural and revealed knowledge must differ from each other. A difference between the two systems arises—1. from the instruction by revelation being subsequent in order, and presupposing that by experience—2. from the different forms of the two communications—the difference considered between an instruction by words and one by signs—the former more adapted for conveying a clear divine knowledge—whilst its comparative limitation directs it to points of high importance—3. from the different ends primarily pursued in each instruction—temporal good, the primary end of our natural instruction—spiritual good, the primary end of revealed instruction—whilst each, in a secondary manner, is subservient to the end of the other.—The two systems of divine instruction differing in the degree in which they evidence the laws of the divine procedure, it becomes necessary, in applying common principles to them, to make allowances for the peculiar circumstances of each system.—Hence it is inferred that their agreement is that of analogy.—Analogy the means of stating a general truth as it may be modified by different circumstances.—The variations under which analogy exhibits a general truth of divine providence, inferred from experience, and applied to the circumstances of the invisible world, may be identified with those allowances, which, taking the doctrines of scripture and facts of nature as our data, we must make on both sides, in order to exhibit them coincident with each other.—To illustrate this, the various ways in which a general principle may be modified by analogy, are considered—1. where the circumstances, from, and to, which we reason, are known to be similar—2. where they are known to be different—3. where their similarity, or difference, cannot be ascertained. This last species of modification is that which belongs to conclusions on subjects of divine revelation, as such conclusions must be held with a reserve for our natural ignorance of the circumstances to which we reason. —But the same consideration of our ignorance obliges us to adopt into such conclusions any particulars of information which an authentic messenger of God may relate to us.— Consequently, on the supposition that the scriptures are authentic, those forms which the laws of Providence may assume in their doctrines, are the real analogies to the facts of nature evidencing the same principles.—This shewn in particular instances of Christian doctrines.—The scriptural account of a future life compared with the notion of a future life inculcated by natural theology—the doctrine of natural theology leads us no further than to the fact, that we may exist through and after death, whereas the scriptures add several particulars—if, however, we have reasoned justly from experience, we have affirmed nothing respecting those points on which the scriptural information is added,—and are open accordingly to the admission of such information, if authentic, into the analogical inference.—The instructions of nature and the scriptures compared as to the doctrine of retribution—nature leading us only to conclude, that it will on the whole be well with the righteous, and ill with the wicked; any particulars respecting the mode or duration of future rewards and punishments are matter of express information, and may therefore, when known, be justly embodied in the analogical inference.—The validity of the analogy between Christianity and nature further pointed out in respect of the circumstantial character of the two instructions —1. as to the circumstance of their exhibiting their respective truths connected in a scheme or constitution—2. as to the circumstance of their containing truths irreconcilable with speculative principles.—That the truths of any two distinct, and yet connected, consecutive, revelations will be analogous, still further illustrated by a comparison of the different parts of Christianity considered as including the Patriarchal, the Jewish, and the Christian dispensations.—The doctrines of scripture then being analogies to the facts of nature, it follows that the evidence resulting to them from their coincidence with these facts is only presumptive—they are proved to be true to a certain extent only, but to their full extent to be like known truths, or to be *as if* they were true.—This evidence may be increased in two ways—either by the accumulation of similar facts in nature evidencing some one principle involved in a doctrine of scripture,—or by the variety of facts evidencing different principles implied in a doctrine—on the other hand, the evidence is diminished by apparent contradictions, or exceptions, in nature, to the operation of a general principle implied in a scriptural truth.—The evidence obtained to the revelation of the scriptures as a whole, not to be estimated by the simple force of particular analogies, as confirmatory of particular doctrines, but by the proof thus derived to the general theory deduced from a collective survey of all the doctrines of the religion.

III. The importance of the credibility resulting from this evidence. 1. Its argumentative force.—It is demonstratively conclusive only on the negative side, as a pretended revelation may perhaps coincide in many respects with nature, and yet be false—irrelevant as an argument in favour of a revelation where there is not the evidence of miracles presupposed—its application as such depends on the importance, extent, and variety of discerned correspondences between a given revelation and the course of nature—where such correspondences are observed, the argument from them to the truth of the revelation is aggravated by the contrast of the two forms of instruction

—it will be further increased if there be any thing in the revelation itself challenging such a scrutiny—that such is the case with regard to Christianity, implied in the precept, to " do the will of God" in order to " know of the doctrine "—also in the tenour of the religion, as a religion which connects its doctrines with the business of human life—which descends to particularities—aspires to reform, not to remodel our nature—connects present and future happiness in the tendency of its system.—The necessity of resorting to the test of experience may also be concluded from a general survey of the Bible as an historical work—the Bible differs not from any other history in its subject-matter, but differs in the peculiar relation under which it contemplates man—whence it follows that its theological instruction is for the most part indirectly conveyed, and not in formal dogmas—its intelligible and practical character results from this mode of instruction, and such a character implies its conformity to experience.— The test further required, in the case of Christianity, to shew the real tendency of the religion in opposition to false appearances against it.—If, accordingly, Christianity be proved conformable to nature, we must argue a coincidence of *design*, and not of *result* only, between its system and that of nature, and a design of that magnitude which must be referred to God.—An indirect argument to the truth of Christianity is obtained from the force of the evidence in repelling objections—it shews that the truth of the religion is independent of objections against particular doctrines—the force of the evidence in this point of view has induced some writers to undervalue it as a positive confirmation of religious truth.—2. The practical importance of the evidence.—Religion demands the aid of practical arguments—this evidence, as being conversant about matter of fact, shews the principles of those doctrines to which it applies, in actual operation, and therefore establishes the practical truth of the religion —the application of the principles of daily life to religious ends does not affect their expediency—by the same method the doctrines are shewn to be practicable, since to act upon them appears to be only to *repeat* what we have done before—it is that sort of evidence which is cogent on our conduct, because it enforces a personal application of the religious truth—also peculiarly adapted to the rapid flux of human life, which admits no delay with regard to religion—it is in fact the argument upon which the belief of the generality exclusively rests, and which is the ultimate appeal of the learned inquirer.—3. The illustrative importance of the evidence.—Peculiar need of illustration in subjects of revelation—not only on account of the real mystery, but of the false mysteriousness which attaches to them from our prejudices.—The illustrative force of the evidence arises,—1. from the nature of analogy in general—analogy as a ground of illustration not *essentially* distinct from analogy as a ground of argument—various ways in which analogy throws light on a subject—it unites the pleasure of association—and that of imitation—converts the learner into self-instructor—2. from the peculiar force of analogy when employed in the subject of religion—as rendering religion more intelligible by exhibiting its truths on a reduced scale—conciliating attention to religion by connecting it with the feeling of *home*—counterbalancing the natural prejudice against the miraculous nature of a revelation.

IV. Objections to the application of the evidence considered—the objection that it is hypothetical and illogical removed by the former consideration of the grounds of the evidence—the objection drawn from its supposed insufficiency refuted by Bishop Butler—Other objections are, 1. that it is unnecessary, or that the testimony to the fact of miracles having been performed in proof of the revelation, is the only requisite test of the truth of its doctrines—that this is not the case shewn by a consideration of the case of an eye-witness to the performance of a miracle—a miracle in proof of a divine commission to teach, cannot be rationally believed without concurring appearances of the other attributes of God besides power—this position illustrated by an instance from the gospel history—miracles not *immediately* conclusive *per se* of the truth of the matters attested by them—they must be considered as *moral* acts—still more is confirmatory evidence wanted when the revelation becomes traditional—2. that the employment of this evidence infringes upon the *necessity* of a supernatural revelation—the nature of the evidence of analogy as being only *presumptive* proof, affords an answer to this—it is competent to us, by reference to the principles of our constitution, to trace the limits of our natural knowledge of divine things—the devout Deist compared in relation to revealed knowledge to the devout Jew in relation to the spirituality of the gospel—3. that the evidence derogates from the *authority* of revelation—it may be abused to the destruction of the integrity of scripture—but where rightly used it exacts a rigid adherence to the scriptural doctrines as they are written—the credibility resulting from this evidence distinct from the reasonableness of religion—it is only in investigating the reasonableness of doctrines that there is danger of impairing the scripture authority, whereas this evidence proceeding on facts checks the presumption of curiosity.—Butler's "Analogy" a convincing specimen of the reserve with which it advances—much misconception on this point avoided by reflecting that reason in no case is the teacher of truth, but is *taught* either by nature or by the scripture-revelation, so that faith in the doctrines of scripture, however unapparent to reason without supernatural light, is in the strictest sense an act of reason.—Distinction of the philosophy of Christianity from other sciences.

Recapitulation of the principal points discussed.—In conclusion—the necessity of exploring the evidence for ourselves in order to the proper estimate of it—it appeals to real principles of our nature, and not to fanciful feelings—the rejection of it proves that the infidel is hardened against the voice of nature as well as of divine revelation—it cannot be rejected without denying all final causes, and thus no practical argument for the existence of a Deity would be left—the advocate of the light of nature ought to be à fortiori the advocate of that of grace—the process of collecting this evidence a needful discipline of the mind to the believer, tending to his utmost improvement at once in wisdom and in piety.

AN ESSAY,

ETC.

That a revelation of the divine wisdom must ultimately rest on the credit of miracles wrought in confirmation of it, and thus be received solely on the authority of God, will be readily acknowledged by every one who considers that it is the divinity of the truth so imparted which constitutes its peculiar nature and importance, and that no inferior sanction, therefore, can be interposed between God and the sacred gift.

But as the heavenly treasure is deposited in earthen vessels, and comes not into our hands by immediate donation from the Supreme Giver Himself, a necessity arises of examining into it in that form in which it is presented to our acceptance, lest we mistake the counterfeit of an impious ingenuity for the pure light of divine wisdom, and dishonour God by paying that reverence to the wisdom of man which is transcendantly due to His word alone. Before, therefore, we admit any proposed revelation to be susceptible of that evidence from miracles which invests it with its perfect authority, we must explore its nature from an actual survey of it in all its parts. We must analyse it into the materials of which it consists, and thus either detect the base infusions of human fraud, if there be any latent within it; or trace out, as far as we may be able, the indications of a design and workmanship beyond the scale and the perfection of man; and which may, without derogation from the divine attributes, be ascribed to the Father of Lights and Author of all goodness.

Now there are two ways in which a judgment may be formed respecting the character of any revelation. Either we may judge of it by itself, referring those views of the Divine Being which it unfolds to us to the principles of our moral nature, which is the direct test of its worthiness to be received: or we may judge of it indirectly by comparison with that previous revelation of God which we possess in the natural world. The first mode of inquiry suggests an answer to the question: is it such a revelation as the Divine Being recognized in the dictates of conscience should give? The second mode of inquiry suggests an answer to the question: is it such a revelation as God has *already given?* Ultimately indeed the two questions converge into one, for they both tend to this point, that God *may* have given the particular revelation into which we are inquiring: but in themselves they are really distinct in their end and their process. The first seeks to establish the *morality* of the revelation; the second to establish its *philosophy*. The first proceeds by à priori reasoning, assuming certain principles of divine truth as indisputable, and arguing from these to the necessary character which must belong to the God of the scriptures. The second proceeds by analysis, taking the facts of the natural world and those of the scripture for its data, tracing both to their general laws, and, by their coincidence with each other in such general laws, determining the likelihood that the God of nature is also the God of the scriptures.

It is to this second mode of inquiry into the divinity of the scriptures, as one of the most interesting subjects which can engage our attention, that the present investigation is addressed. It is purposed to examine, first, into the grounds of the credibility thence derived to the Christian revelation; secondly, the nature of that credibility; thirdly, its full importance; and lastly, to consider the force of some objections which may be urged against its application.

It seems almost unnecessary to prove, that the natural world may no less strictly be regarded as a revelation from God than the written word. But as it is upon this assumption that the whole inquiry proceeds—for it would be impossible otherwise to bring into comparison with each other two such incommensurable things, as an inspired book and the created universe,—we should be able to give a reason for this assumption.

And the reason appears to be this: that we find in our minds an evident adaptation to the course of outward nature. The eye is not more adapted by its peculiar structure to the nature of light, nor are the lungs more formed with relation to the atmospheric air, than the principles of our minds are adjusted to the world in which we live and act. Consider only that regularity which obtains in every thing which lives, or moves, or vegetates in the world around us, and how this regularity without us has its counterpart within us, in that principle of our minds which leads us to place an habitual dependence on the continuance of such regularity, a principle which is the basis of all our calculations and reasonings, and in short of our whole conduct in life*. All our knowledge indeed is the

---

* A question may be raised, " whether this principle of our minds, whereby we rely upon the continuance and regularity of the laws of nature, be an original impression, or a result of repeated experience, which begins to confide because it sees no cause to mistrust."—The *knowledge* of the existence of this principle in our minds, is matter of experience; our finding that things do proceed in a certain course, gives occasion to the developement of the principle and consequent knowledge

result of this adjustment of the principles of our minds to our condition, since it is the percep- of its existence. But the fact of its existence, as distinct from our knowledge of it, antecedently to experience, is plain from the confidence with which children repose on testimony; that confidence, evidently, not being *formed* by any experience of the uniform nature of testimony, but being *corrected* and *regulated* by experience, which teaches us to restrict our natural tendency to an implicit credit. An inexperienced or an untutored person wonders at many events which the experienced or instructed sees no reason to wonder at: that is, he is startled at finding this principle of his mind not answered in every instance by an uniformity in external nature; whereas the latter finds a solution of the difficulty from his knowledge of the *more* general laws of nature, under which he is enabled to range the phenomena which perplex the former, and begins to wonder rather at that uniformity of nature in which he before unsuspectingly acquiesced. "When I was young", observes Dr. Hey, " I felt no surprise at the return of the summer or winter; and I imagine, the unthinking peasant takes all usual changes in natural phenomena as things of course; but now, the days never grow longer in spring without exciting in my mind a pretty strong sentiment of wonder or admiration: and even in those instances in which I reflect the least, I should be less struck with a *real* change of what we call the Laws of Nature, than a peasant would be, though he would believe accounts of things supernatural sooner than I should. . . . . Improvements in knowledge and reasoning

tion of facts *as they appear* to minds constituted as the human mind is.

If then a divine Author be acknowledged at once of nature and of the mind of man, we cannot do otherwise than assign, as the final cause, the instruction which results from this admirable adjustment. And the whole course of nature accordingly, so long as the mind of man is what it is, cannot but be considered in the light of a revelation from God.

I. Regarding then the natural world as a

make real violations of laws of nature more easily admitted, not less easily."—Hey's Lectures in Divinity, Vol. I. p. 164. So again in the study of religion the child of the world, he who judges by the unchastened principles of his nature, discovers, as he thinks, contrarieties to the order of Providence in the intimations of scripture; he wonders that his principles of expectation should be disappointed: but as he becomes more instructed unto the kingdom of heaven, and puts away childish things, he is more and more placed beyond the reach of such disappointment by learning to restrict the application of the principles of his nature within their proper limits.

" Intellectus humanus *ex proprietate sua* facile supponit majorem ordinem et æqualitatem in rebus quàm invenit", &c.—Nov. Organum, I. 45.

kind of revelation from God, have we any reason to think that there must be an evident agreement between the instruction supernaturally conveyed and attested by miracles, and that which is placed within the reach of our faculties? To decide this question, is to point out the grounds of that credibility which the scriptures derive from their comparison with the book of nature; or, in other words, the foundation of that analogy which is asserted between revealed religion and the course and constitution of the world.

Now we have a general presumption that there must exist some points of coincidence in the truths unfolded by the scriptures, and those taught by the experienced course of nature, from that very repugnance which we feel to admit a scriptural revelation, on account of its departure from the established method of divine providence in its mode of instruction; and which induces us to seek anxiously for some redeeming probabilities in its internal character.

It would be difficult to account for the backwardness of men to believe in the scriptures on account of their miraculous character, unless there were real ground for that expectation of conformity with known truth which the mind so naturally forms. As an immediate revelation from Heaven is miraculous in the very notion of it, to demand the evidence of probability in its favour appears to be a forgetfulness of its proper nature; and yet a demand so generally felt cannot be considered as unreasonable:—there must be, it would seem, some real ground for a repugnance which acts in many cases as an obstacle to the reception of the truth revealed—some means of converting its apparent hostility into a real advocacy of the truth, by shewing how it may be satisfied without derogating from the miraculous nature of the scriptures.

Antecedently moreover to any distinct examination of the real state of the case, we may reasonably suspect from the analogy of our knowledge in general, that there must exist some tie of connexion between the facts of our experience, and the truths communicated by immediate revelation. Whilst we observe that mutual respect and subserviency which bind together the various departments of mere human knowledge, however distinct and independent of each other in their peculiar pursuits, we are led to think that the divine science of the word of God cannot be found, when rightly estimated, to be a knowledge detached from all communion and sympathy with the science of nature, or the truths inculcated on our minds by observation of the course and constitution of the world.

But then, on the other hand, presumptions adverse to such a coincidence are suggested from the evidently vast difference between the knowledge revealed by the scriptures and that naturally acquired both in the form of communication, and the sublimer nature of the subjects about which the scriptures are conversant; the scriptures being a direct message from God, nature only appearing to be such indirectly; the scriptures discoursing to us of the future and the invisible world, nature apparently limiting its information to the things present and visible.

The question then recurs, whether there are

any just media of comparison, by which the two classes of truths may be brought to the test of their agreement or disagreement with each other, so that the unseen truth may obtain a credibility from its coincidence with that which is matter of experience. It is clear that, however great the difference may be in the form and subjects of the two communications, there can be no disagreement between them; from the general consideration, that both are equally the appointed instructions of the same divine Author. Any express contradiction between their respective assertions would argue either a diversity of authorship, or imperfection in a single author. And accordingly as the knowledge acquired from nature is the first in order, and what we cannot but believe according to the principles of our constitution; in the event of a contradiction, we must reject the pretended revelation as internally convicted of falsehood.

The same conclusion may be drawn also from the consideration, that both kinds of instruction are addressed to the same human nature.

The same moral and intellectual faculties by

which one class of truths is received and adopted, must hold good also when applied to the other class; and no judgment therefore affirmed in the system of nature can be reversed in the system of grace: for this would imply one mode of thinking and feeling to be applied to one kind of instruction, and another to the other.

In the event of a contradiction therefore, the revelation in question must, for the same reasons as before, be discarded as unworthy of credit. But though we may thus certainly conclude, that there can be no disagreement in the respective voices of nature and the scriptures, it does not appear from such considerations, that there must be any implicit agreement between them.

They may still be conceived to be so distinct in their peculiar truths, that whilst there is no contradiction between them, there is no possibility of coming even to a negative decision respecting the credibility of the scriptures; so far as their credibility may depend on a presumed necessity of their coincidence with experience. What we want then is, a proof of the necessary existence of some common principles equally belonging to our natural and scriptural instructions, without which the pretension to inspiration must be false; but which, by their presence, shall bestow a strong probability, that the scriptures were, as they aspire to be considered, the inditings of the same Spirit who speaks to us by the unambiguous oracle of our experience. Let us examine therefore whether it be not necessary that the scriptures, or rather any volume which claims to be a record of divine truth, *agree essentially* (however sublime its theme may be) with the lessons which we learn from the natural world.

Here we might refer to the words of the son of Sirach, who declares, speaking of the works of God, " all things are double, one against another, and He hath made nothing imperfect"*; and to the still more express and familiar passage of St. Paul, in which it is said, that " the invisible things of God from the creation of the world are clearly seen, being understood by the things that are made, even his eternal power

* Eccl^{cus}. xlii. 24.

and god-head"*; in both which assertions, the existence is implied of some common principles of truth in the systems of nature and grace: but our object is to ascertain the foundation on which these assertions rest.

The difficulty which arises on this point is from the sublimity and remoteness of the subjects about which a revelation immediately vouchsafed from Heaven is conceived to be conversant; since these are conceived to be so completely out of the verge of human speculation, as to preclude the application to them of any common principles derived from our experience. Now in one sense this is true, and in

---

* Rom. i. 20. It is not meant to affirm that St. Paul expressly asserts in this passage a correspondence between the scripture revelation and nature. His words, it is evident, refer exclusively to the instruction of nature. It is only meant, that his assertion respecting this instruction of nature *pre-supposes* a fundamental agreement between scriptural and natural theology—that nature taught the same essential truth which was orally delivered to the hearers of the word preached, so that the Heathen were placed in a like situation as to *kind*, though not as to degree, of religious knowledge, with the Christian convert.

another false. If it be understood as pointing out the impropriety of applying common principles to matters of fact and truths of inspiration, with confidence in the mode of the application, it is true; because we then proceed on the hypothesis that we are equally acquainted with the nature of the case in each system. But if it is construed to mean, that common principles do not *exist* in both systems, the position is false; for the same principles may exist in both, notwithstanding our utter uncertainty in their application from the visible to the invisible world. The fact of their *existence* is all that our present inquiry demands.

It being conceded then that the voice of inspired wisdom must communicate to us truths concerning God (for we can conceive no other knowledge but religion, worthy of His special interposition to teach, or rather His speaking to us by revelation is religious instruction in itself), which human wisdom in its utmost agony of thought could never have discovered, or at least ascertained; it may still be maintained, that there will be an intercommunity of sentiment between the heavenly and the earthly messengers of truth, and that the true philosophy of nature will be found also the philosophy of the sublimest religion.

The question turns entirely, not upon the *quantity* of information which may be conveyed by an inspired messenger from God, but on the *nature* of it; for if the knowledge of divine things should be of a different nature in each system, there could be no means of comparing the two systems; but if they are necessarily of the same nature, then, however the knowledge which is of grace may surpass that which is learned by experience, the two systems of divinity must *essentially* agree in some common principles.

Now all our knowledge of God by experience, is confessedly relative in its nature. That it is such, is implied in the very terms which enuntiate it as the knowledge of experience. We acquire our natural knowledge of His existence from a consciousness of our own existence; for this consciousness is the basis even of all our reasonings à priori concerning His being and attributes; we acknowledge His intellectual and moral attributes by conceiving principles in Him, corresponding to the principles in ourselves which produce moral and intellectual effects; his power, in like manner, by transferring to Him unlimited superiority of energy and dominion, such as are exercised among men. Thus we know Him only by reflection. We can apply our experience with confidence of knowledge when we extend its conclusions from ourselves to our fellow-creatures, because " as in water face answereth to face, so the heart of man to man" : though even here it may be questioned whether our conviction of a moral identity of nature is founded on any higher proof than that which results from an observation of their manner of acting. But we cannot regard our experience as an absolute authority, when we look beyond ourselves to Him whose infinity of nature constitutes an unparalleled case. We cannot therefore consider our natural knowledge of God as more than relative. It implies the real existence of principles in the nature of the Deity, correspondent to the principles in the nature of man which produce similar effects; but as obtained from observation, it is necessarily qualified by the character and circumstances of the observer *.

But are we capable of attaining to a knowledge of God different in kind from this, by means of the illuminating grace of the Holy Spirit shed abroad in the scriptures of truth?— From the following considerations, it will appear that no scriptural revelation—that is, no revelation which is not imparted at once to the mind by direct inspiration—can introduce to the understanding of man a higher kind of knowledge. Our natural divine knowledge will be corrected, confirmed, and enlarged in degree,

---

* See Archbishop King's " Discourse on Predestination, with Notes by Dr. Whately." Bishop Browne's " Procedure, Extent, and Limits of Human Understanding", and " Things Divine and Supernatural, conceived by Analogy with Things Natural and Human." Dr. Copleston's " Enquiry into the Doctrines of Necessity and Predestination", Disc. III. with the Notes: and Dr. Whately's " Essays on some of the Peculiarities of the Christian Religion", Essay V.

by any authentic light from Heaven; but it will still remain relative in kind.

1. This limitation of the knowledge communicable by an inspired messenger may be inferred from the fixed standard of those faculties to which it is addressed. Those faculties are conformed in their structure to that natural vehicle of knowledge which the world presents. In the world they are to be exercised, and it is, therefore, necessary that they should be adapted to that scene of things about which they are conversant. If they had been so framed by the Divine Artificer, as to perceive and know independently of experience, the principles of the knowledge so acquired would not have admitted of a ready application to the circumstances of the world. That knowledge only which is furnished by experience, is fitted for reaction in the emergencies of human life; for the mode of application is also learned together with the learning itself. Had the faculties of man, accordingly, been made so powerful as to apprehend the things of the world by simple intuition; though they had attained to a higher knowledge

and accomplished their purpose with greater facility, they would have been incapacitated for the acquirement of that dexterity in the use of the things of the world which experience gives. Being furnished with principles of truth, not from an observation of effects, but independently of the actual phenomena of nature—as instruments, they would have been too keen for the purposes for which they were immediately required.—The standard of our faculties being thus fixed by their necessary relation to their sphere of operation, any message from God must, in order to be intelligible, conform its instructions to the existing standard. It cannot impart to them a knowledge of a different nature from that which they are adapted to receive; and this we find to be of a relative nature; such therefore must be also the truth scripturally revealed.

2. If we further consider that human ideas and language are the instruments which must be employed in a scriptural revelation, we shall readily perceive that it cannot acquaint us with divine things otherwise than consistently with

those principles of theological truth which are collected from observation of the natural world. Though its tree of knowledge may be a plant of the heavenly paradise, and may bear aloft on its branches the golden fruits of its native clime; still it must strike its roots in the earth, and clothe itself with a foliage congenial to its adopted soil. For the very act of enlightening the mind with extraordinary truth, presupposes the acquisition of some previous knowledge, as the substratum and element of that sublimer truth which it purposes to teach. Without some natural apprehension of the being and attributes of God, a discourse of His mysterious providences would but amaze and bewilder the reason of man. However fraught with divine wisdom, yet, like the fabled music of the spheres, its strains could not be heard by mortal ear. Whilst therefore a light from Heaven may extend our natural notions of divine things in the highest degree, and in the greatest variety of particulars, it cannot introduce to the mind ideas concerning them, essentially different from all that it ever entered into the heart of man to conceive.

These are those secrets of the Lord which it belongs to a more spiritualized state of existence to disclose to human apprehension. At present we can only hear of God, even through his special messengers, in our own tongue wherein we were born. Those modes of thought which we have acquired in the course of our natural education, are the universal language, into which a scriptural revelation must translate its most recondite mysteries. They are our schoolmasters, which bring us to the knowledge of revealed religion. Thus, when Christianity unfolds to us the high mystery of a Trinity in the Unity of the Divine Nature, it enlarges our knowledge of God to a degree beyond the ken of human intellect, but still the ideas upon which that sublime information is grounded, are all of a relative character. It is still a relative Deity whom it reveals to us, when we learn that there are three Persons in the Unity of the Godhead: for it is only from being enabled to behold God in the new distinct relations of a Redeemer and a Sanctifier, superadded to that in which we naturally regard him as our Father in heaven, that we are led to the confession of the co-equal Godhead of the Son and the Holy Ghost. We know much more accordingly of God in *degree* by this supernatural information, but our knowledge of Him remains the same in *kind*.

3. Supposing, however, that the Scriptures could dispense with our preliminary natural knowledge of divine things, we shall arrive at the same conclusion respecting the nature of their communications, from the fact alone, that they employ the instrumentality of language in conveying their instruction. For what is it to teach by language, but to teach by ideas which are already part of the stock of human knowledge? New, and otherwise undiscoverable, appropriations of our natural ideas may be suggested by language consecrated to the office of interpreting the counsels of the Most High; but still the original sense of the words employed must be the basis of the imposed theological sense. Thus the terms, by which our minds are led to the perception of unknown truths concerning God, are necessarily analogical: they express the ideas of which they are the signs, but those

ideas, at the same time, in a new and peculiar acceptation, derived from the subjects to which they are transferred. By this application of language we are made acquainted with facts concerning God, without any fundamental alteration of our original conceptions. By the employment of the terms in an authentic revelation we know assuredly that there must be real principles of the divine nature, and real acts of God, correspondent to the principles and acts of human life signified by the terms so adopted in the message from Heaven. We know, for instance, certainly, that there is that in the nature of God, which will prompt him to reward and punish mankind according to the rules of distributive justice, because we are assured of the fact, in terms which we fully understand; though the terms themselves impart to us no intimate knowledge of his nature. We know again, that there are three persons in the Godhead, as far as the existence of the fact so revealed is concerned, because we read the fact in the pages of Scripture; but we do not know that the notion of personality, under which the triune nature of God is revealed, is strictly appropriate, abstractedly from the circumstances of the human intellect, though it points to an indisputable truth, latent, as it were, under it, concerning the divine nature.

In this respect, indeed, it is with theology, as with all other sciences. All that any human science justly aspires to teach, is an accurate and comprehensive knowledge of the particular facts in that department of nature which is the field of its investigation, and not an acquaintance with the essential nature of the subjects. When Natural Philosophy instructs us in the existence of an universal law of gravitation, it furnishes us with a general fact, under which all the particular phenomena in the motions of bodies may be classed, but it does not attempt to explain to us the nature of the force of gravity*. So also theology, while discoursing to us

---

* " Videmus tantum corporum figuras et colores; audimus tantum sonos; tangimus tantum superficies externas; olfacimus odores solos; et gustamus sapores; intimas substantias nullo sensu, nulla actione reflexa cognoscimus; et multo minus ideam habemus substantiæ Dei." Newt. Princip. III. Schol.

in human accents of the things pertaining to the kingdom of God, confines its intimations to a knowledge of the bare facts which it unfolds, leaving us to dwell with awful wonder, and faith, and piety, on the sacred mysteries, whose existence it satisfactorily vouches to us, but cannot explain.

The knowledge of God accordingly conveyed by the Scriptures, being of the same kind as that collected from nature, it follows that there must be some common principles of theology pervading the systems of grace and nature. This leads us to inquire more closely what these principles are.

Now the only conceivable end of instruction from God is the good of mankind. "He hath shewed thee, O man, what is good, for what doth the Lord require of thee, but to do justly, and to love mercy, and to walk humbly with thy God?" may be inscribed as its motto on any authentic record of the divine will. For it is plainly unreasonable to suppose, that religious doctrines can be revealed, to be held merely as *credenda*, as truths which ought to be received without reference to conduct : since a theoretic life is evidently not the perfect state of a being furnished with active principles; and a religion, accordingly, which provided us only with materials of intellectual enjoyment, would be insufficient for the purposes of human nature, and would carry its own condemnation in its manifest deficiency. The Scriptures of truth therefore will supply motives as well as convictions; not opinions only, but rules of duty. The sublimest doctrines contained in them will all have a practical tendency, bearing on the heart no less than on the understanding.

The fact is, there can be no knowledge merely speculative on the subjects of religion; whether obtained from the course of the world, or from the Scriptures. Relations to the Deity, and to the future invisible world, however made known to the mind of man, so far as they are really believed, must have their influence on human conduct. As we cannot learn under the natural tuition of experience, that God is our Creator and Governor, without an accompanying sense of duties resulting from this knowledge; so it is impossible for us to learn from the Scriptures that God is our Redeemer and our Sanctifier, without feeling corresponding obligations immediately rush upon our minds as the living, energizing representatives of the faith which is in us. Let us be only fully convinced, that our present life is the beginning of an eternal duration; and how irresistibly are we urged to a mode of conduct, answerable to that accession of importance, which our present condition in the world derives from the peculiar point of view in which we then contemplate it!

This obligation of religious truth to condescend to the wants of mankind, must have its effect on the nature of the truth imparted. If the doctrines taught supernaturally are to be practically brought home to us, or are necessarily influential on our conduct, they must be of such a nature as readily to combine with those natural principles of action which are inculcated on us by the course and constitution of the world. For it is by these principles, instilled into us by the droppings of time, which have imperceptibly worked their way into our minds, growing with our growth, and strengthening with our strength, that our conduct will ultimately be regulated, notwithstanding any fuller information respecting our duties subsequently delivered. These are laws written in our hearts, learned by dint of our very constitution: whereas the motives derived from Scriptural truth are received in the first place as laws of positive institution, and are afterwards discerned in their moral force. If the doctrines, accordingly, of the Scriptures did not harmonize with our natural principles of action, but taught a system of theology altogether abhorrent from them, they would reach the heart too late to establish their empire there, when the ground was already preoccupied by the aboriginal productions of the soil.

In order then that the practical obligations resulting from our natural and scriptural knowledge of divine things may not interfere and clash with each other, it is further necessary, whilst both oracles of truth impart a relative knowledge of God, that they should implicitly agree in unfolding the same general principles of the divine administration. For what else is the instruction of nature, when considered in its practical force, but general views of the divine conduct translated into general rules of human life? All things having been ordered for the best under the providence of a wise, and good, and powerful God, a conformity with the proper course of natural events must be the sure and only means of attaining to that good, to which the excellent order of the universe is directed. But it is not the course of natural events, as they appear to the eye of superficial observation, encumbered and impeded with the accidental circumstances of an apostate world, which gives the true outline and form of that providence which sustains it; but it is their real tendency, abstractedly from those noxious incrustations, deposited, as it were, around the fact of nature by the turbid stream of the world, which is the truth as it is of God. The mind, therefore, in the very act of learning from experience, is compelled to generalize the particular facts submitted to its observation, and thus explores the laws of nature, or, in other words, general principles of the divine administration, as its rules of action. Nor is this analytical process carried on in the mind of the philosopher alone, who studies the system of natural theology: but the common man, who requires the knowledge thence derived for the purposes of life, as much as the philosopher requires it for the purposes of science, has a capacity for it, in the adaptation itself of the human mind to the condition of the world; and thus, unconsciously to himself, philosophizes in secret concerning the facts of his observation *. So it is also with respect to the doctrines of Scripture. Practically considered they resolve themselves into general

---

* The faculty of generalizing is that which distinguishes reason from brute instinct. Without it we should only apprehend and know things according to their gross appearances. But that exercise of it in which it eminently appears as the proprium of man, is when it is employed upon actions as such, in selecting out of events those qualities which constitute virtuousness or viciousness in them. "It does not appear," observes Bishop Butler, "that brutes have the least reflex sense of actions as distinguished from events; or that will and design, which constitute the very nature of actions as such, are at all an object to their perception." Diss. on the Nature of Virtue, p. 434. Bishop Hallifax's Ed.

views of the divine procedure presented for the guidance of human conduct. In applying any scriptural truth to the purposes of our life, we examine the principles of action involved in it. As being a relative information concerning God, it represents to us God acting in some way towards ourselves: and we, accordingly, explore that way, that by acting ourselves in conformity with it, we may, as it were, express the doctrine in our lives. This appears to be the process by which a revelation of mysterious truth is practically received, and converted to the benefit of mankind.

Hence, though the holiest truths concerning God, and the world beyond our view, may be written in the volume of inspirations, and appear resplendent amidst its more homely themes—as the gold amidst the other riches of some lordly treasure—yet will not even such abstruse doctrines be without some principle of connexion with the instructions of the natural world. The same plan of divine providence will be found pervading both the miraculous and natural admonitions of God to man, as the primary rule of both, forming an indissoluble tie of consanguinity between them, and proclaiming the same ultimate origin to the wisdom which " crieth without, and uttereth her voice in the streets", and the wisdom which is the daughter of inspiration.

Those general principles, accordingly, of the divine procedure, which, God being conceded to be the author of nature, must exist in the systems of nature and grace, are the legitimate media by which the truths of scripture may be brought into comparison with the facts of the natural world; and a coincidence in which is absolutely necessary in order to the credibility of the doctrines revealed. It is with reference to these media of comparison that Bishop Butler observes*, that " it must be allowed just to join abstract reasonings with the observation of facts, and argue from such facts as are known, to others that are like them; from that part of the divine government over intelligent creatures which comes under our view, to that larger and

---

* Introduction to The Analogy, p. 7. Butler's Works.

more general government which is beyond it, and from what is present, to collect what is likely, credible, or not incredible, will be hereafter."

II. In proceeding to consider the nature of the credibility thus derived to scriptural truth, it is necessary to inquire into those peculiarities by which our natural and scriptural instructions are distinguished from each other, and which must necessarily preclude an entire agreement between them. These peculiarities may be traced to the distinct forms of the two communications, and the purposes to which they are primarily directed; as from their characteristic differences in these respects, a difference in the truths respectively imparted by them, will necessarily result.

1. That the scriptures will convey a knowledge to man of a much more exalted and comprehensive character than that which he acquires from observation of the course of the natural world, is sufficiently apparent from the fact that their truths are engrafted on those of

experience. An instruction expressly given subsequently, and in addition to the stores of uninspired wisdom, implies a superiority in itself to the knowledge which it assumes as its foundation. It would be superfluous, if it contained nothing more than what mankind already possessed through the ordinary channel of their experience. Nor can we suppose that a departure would be made from the ordinary means of communication employed by the Creator in conveying his will to his creatures, and that so stupendous a series of miraculous interpositions, as those embodied in the scripture narratives, would be exhibited, merely to repeat and confirm the law of nature. Something more than the truth as taught by nature appears therefore to be necessarily involved in the notion of a miraculous revelation.

2. But let us consider the effect which the peculiar *form* of each communication will have on the truths made known. God, when he instructs us by the word of his Spirit, employs the conventional signs of ideas already acquired by the mind. When he instructs us by objects and

events presented to our observation, he speaks in that universal language which preceded all utterance of human tongue,—that language whose accents were heard, when first the creation arose in all its glories, when " the morning stars sang together, and all the sons of God shouted for joy."

The scriptures indeed exhibit an union of both these methods of instruction. They give us an account of symbolical actions, as well as words, employed on some occasions for the purpose of revealing the will of God*.

* " I have also spoken by the Prophets, and I have multiplied visions, and used similitudes by the ministry of the Prophets." Hosea, xii. 10. The prophet Ezekiel is the great exemplar of the mixed mode of divine instruction. See also Jotham's parable of "the trees." Judges, ix. 7. Jeremiah, xiii. 1. xxiv. 1. xxxv. 1. Amos, vii. 7. viii. 1. And the account of Agabus binding his hands and feet with Paul's girdle, and saying, "Thus saith the Holy Ghost; so shall the Jews at Jerusalem bind the man that owneth this girdle, and shall deliver him into the hands of the Gentiles." Acts, xxi. 11.

The use of types under the preparatory dispensation of Judaism, in which they served as subordinate means of divine instruction, accords with the view here taken of the signs of God in nature. The full revelation to which that partial sys-

Such was the language of the types of the Mosaic covenant, and of the various ceremonies of

tem was introductory, would have been anticipated out of season, if the types had conveyed a clear information on the subjects of which they were significant. The employment of symbolical language in prophecy answered in like manner the purpose of casting a necessary obscurity over the events foreshewn. The parables of our Lord may also be referred to as illustrative of the defectiveness of the language of events in itself. Their character as vehicles of divine knowledge is thus expressed by Saint Matthew: "All these things spake Jesus unto the multitude in parables, and without a parable spake he not unto them; that it might be fulfilled which was spoken by the prophet, saying, I will open my mouth in parables; I will utter things which have been kept secret from the foundation of the world."—Matthew, xiii. 34, 35. And more pointedly by Saint Mark; " Unto you it is given to know the mystery of the kingdom of God, but unto them that are without, all these things are done in parables; that seeing they may see and not perceive, and hearing they may hear and not understand."—Mark, iv. 11, 12. To this veiled character of parabolical instruction refers that earnest call to attention, with which the delivery of it was sometimes accompanied; " He that hath ears to hear, let him hear." At the same time parables as means of instruction concerning human conduct, are the most simple and interesting lessons. For instance, the parable of Nathan was the readiest mode of flash-

the law. Such was Jonah's miraculous deliverance; such was the vision of the sheet, de-

ing conviction of sin on the mind of the offending king. It is as vehicles of theological truth that they are less clear than more direct statements. There is, however, something of obscurity in them, even when only morally applied, as it is by an after-thought that their practical application is discovered. David first condemned the guilty individual of the parable, and then himself. There is also a considerable difference in degree of clearness between a parable, as an event described, and an instructive event simply witnessed; inasmuch as a parable is explained in some measure by the person and circumstances of the relator, if not by its connexion with the rest of his discourse.

That events are naturally regarded as possible means of information appears from the reliance placed on omens, and the appearances of the animals offered in sacrifice in ancient times. The custom of demanding earth and water of a people as tokens of their subjection, is an instance of the use of symbolical language. Tarquin's reply to his son by striking off the heads of the poppies in the garden (Liv. i. 54.); that of Thrasybulus to Periander of a similar kind (Herodot. Terps. 92.); the Scythian king's present to Darius of "a bird, a mouse, a frog, and five arrows" (Herodot. Melp. 131.); the successful device of the Samian ambassadors in carrying an empty sack round the Spartan assembly to indicate their want of succour (Herodot. Thal. 46.); are all instances to the same

claring to Saint Peter the admission of the Gentiles into the divine favour; such was the impressive event of our Lord's transfiguration; the withering of the fig-tree as indicating the

effect. The Egyptian hieroglyphics will readily occur to every one as illustrations of this mode of teaching, as well as the picture-writing of the Mexicans described by Robertson in his America, Book V. Vol. II. p. 263.

Infidels have endeavoured to represent the transaction of our Lord's washing the feet of his disciples as entitled to be considered sacramental no less than Baptism and the Lord's Supper. And there have been Christians who have thought that we should literally imitate this action of our Lord. Barclay, the apologist of Quakerism, argues from it against the sacraments. But there is evidently no inward grace attached to the outward act. Saint Peter appears to have supposed that there was; but our Lord's final explanation removes any such misapprehension. It is nothing more than a *significant* action.

The double sense of prophecy sufficed to the like purpose, as when the first intention of the prophecy was accomplished, the event so fulfilled was at once an earnest of a further fulfilment, and a foreshewing by visible signs of the ultimate application.

See the remarks of Dr. Hey, on the subject of this note, in his Lectures in Divinity, Vol. I. p. 227 and 252; and Warburton's Div. Legat. Book VI. Sec. 5.

corresponding withering of the Jewish polity; and that significant action used by our Lord, when he instructed his disciples in the humiliating spirit of his religion, by washing their feet. Such is the tone of the whole book of the Apocalypse.

But this method of instruction by symbolical actions as exhibited in the scriptures, is adopted rather as an energetic and striking accompaniment of the word preached, than as an entire substitute for it; and presupposes a living authoritative expounder of the divine will, to interpret and apply it in its full force. The particular instances, in fact, in which such a mode of teaching was employed, had a subserviency to the particular oral revelation, with which they were associated, corresponding to that which the whole natural world, as an organ of divine instruction, has to a scriptural revelation in general.

Now the difference between the scriptural and the symbolical language of the Deity consists in this: that the former gives us the precise ideas without the intervention of our senses;

the latter requires the previous processes of perception and judgment. When our Lord washed the feet of his disciples, Saint Peter questioned him concerning the action, "Lord, dost thou wash my feet?" Jesus answered and said unto him, "what I do thou knowest not now, but thou shalt know hereafter." Here we find an action performed full of sacred meaning, and yet that meaning was hidden to those who witnessed it. Saint Peter looked only to the condescension of the act itself, and deemed it unworthy of his blessed Master. He stopped short of the divine import afterwards made known in the words of Jesus; "Know ye what I have done to you? ye call me Master and Lord, and ye say well, for so I am; if I then, your Lord and Master, have washed your feet, ye also ought to wash one another's feet. For I have given you an example, that ye should do as I have done to you." An instruction by actions or events may appear accordingly to rest in itself, or to have accomplished its purpose in the mere perception of it, as this particular act of our Lord appeared to Saint Peter nothing more than an office unworthy of his Master: or it may be misconstrued from the judgment not being rightly exercised about it; as on this same occasion, Saint Peter, on being corrected by our Lord for his insensibility to the religious nature of the act, erroneously conceived it to convey a mystical purification, or to be sacramental in its character; as is indicated by his answer; " Lord, not my feet only, but also my hands and my head." Every event considered as a means of divine instruction, thus, either is without meaning, or is ambiguous; and is therefore, when alone, that is, without verbal instruction accompanying it, unadapted for conveying any information concerning God, except the most simple and elementary, such as the knowledge of his being and attributes. Upon these fundamental points, God has not left himself without a clear witness, so that perhaps there are no truths which so force themselves upon the understanding as those relating to his providence. But for the plainness of our natural instruction on these points no revelation of more intimate truths could have been authenticated to us. This seems to be the reason of their being made to stand forth so prominently in the page of nature.

If man were perfect in his moral and intellectual powers, as when first he came forth from the hands of his Creator, it might be conceived that the language of nature would have clearly and infallibly conveyed to his understanding and heart that knowledge of God which was requisite for his duty and his happiness; so far at least as the creation was appointed by God in the stead of more express revelation. He would have seen the traces of the Almighty agent, not as now, through the obscurations of a perverse and blind understanding, but with a quick and lively perception*. But, however this may be,

---

* It is not however asserted, that a revelation by words, or by direct inspiration, was not necessary for man even in his perfect state of being. Supernatural instruction may have formed an original essential part in the scheme by which God designed to impart wisdom to man. We may at the same time see a *reason* for such a kind of instruction after the fall, but none for concluding that it was necessary before. It is only as seeing a sufficient reason, according to human apprehension, for a divine interposition, that we can justly assert the *necessity* of an express revelation at any given period.

his fall has evidently destroyed the keenness of his moral eye—he has no longer an ear for the melody of the creation—and he must now collect by slow process of reasoning amidst doubting and suspicion of error, the truths which otherwise would have immediately told their own tale in all their native charm.

In the lapsed state of man, accordingly, a revelation in words becomes more especially necessary for the direct and clear communication of the will of God, in order to human happiness. Though more limited, it should seem, in its nature than a revelation by the works of God—(for, in employing words, it must be so far restricted to the use of such signs as have been adopted into the use of mankind for the communication of their ideas to each other, whereas the signs which the universe presents are in themselves without limit,)—yet it is more expedient for arresting the attention of mankind, and impressing with the stamp of authority on their minds the truths which belong to their peace. The knowledge of Him which His works present is sufficient to leave men without excuse, if they do not love and obey Him: but the knowledge given by a scriptural revelation is so direct and explicit, that man cannot but hear and understand, and be converted by it, unless he wilfully stops his ears to the truth, and will not understand, that he may be converted and live. The imperfection of language, as an instrument of thought, must have some influence in retarding the reception of the divine instructions, and obscuring their meaning; more particularly as those languages in which they may have been originally given become more ancient; but still a communication by words is unquestionably, in the present condition of the world, the most direct and unexceptionable means of imparting divine truth to the mind. The same perverseness indeed of human nature, which deadens our faculties to the appeal of the creation, must operate to the prejudice of scriptural truth, and cause it, in like manner, to bear no meaning to the mind in some cases, in others, to be misconceived and misrepresented. And yet, notwithstanding the dullness of the ignorant, the apathy of the indifferent, the contradictions of the proud and rebellious understanding, the sacred truth consigned to faithful records remains in all its integrity and prominence, to such as will impartially and diligently address themselves to the inquiry after it. In the scriptures it is to be found, as the pure ore collected and refined for our immediate use. It is so set forth in those lively oracles as to be readily accessible to all—so that our Lord's expression where he says, " the words which I speak unto you, they are spirit and they are life", may truly be extended to the whole volume of inspirations.

A revelation by words being a more direct and impressive mode of communication from God, the substance of the instruction conveyed by it will consequently be at once of a more distinct and sublime character than that acquired by the medium of the natural world. Truths, which reason would never have discerned, if left to make its own inferences from the facts of experience, will appear disclosed to our view, as we follow the written guidance of the Spirit, with a vividness of colouring which belongs to objects placed in the foreground of a landscape. As the art of the painter selects out of the mass of objects presented in a survey of nature the most interesting for representation on the canvas, so the pencil of sacred delineation sketches those forms of the spiritual world with its boldest touches, which are the highest in theological interest. The very limitation imposed on it by the materials employed, may reasonably be supposed to cause its attention to be directed to the communication of such truths as are essentially important for man to know; and that such truths, accordingly, will be selected as the proper subjects of any authentic scriptural revelation, and enforced on the notice of mankind with all the copiousness and sublimity of divine eloquence.

3. But it will more distinctly appear, from considering what must be the primary purpose of a scriptural revelation, that its truths must be fraught more richly with the treasures of heavenly knowledge, than those with which our experience of natural providence acquaints us.

Whilst nature abounds with theological instruction, yet instruction of such a kind is not its immediate and primary business. Its lessons, as conjointly derived from the principles of our constitution and that condition in which we have been placed, are, on that account, peculiarly adapted for reaction on those circumstances which have given them their mould. A knowledge of the principles of our minds, and of the laws by which the world is governed, must, in the first place, find its application in the purposes of our present being. Hence it may be concluded, that the immediate end of our instruction by the course of nature, is, that we may obtain our natural good as inhabitants of this world.

The scriptures, on the contrary, are a direct appeal to God himself and the things of the invisible world. As a miraculous communication, they proclaim that their tidings are extraordinary—that they are conversant about things beyond the proper attestation of the ordinary course of nature. They call upon us to give ear to the Almighty Lord of heaven and earth, and to seek a more intimate acquaintance with Him. The spiritual good of man, accordingly, is their primary object. By bringing down God to our contemplation, not only as he is the disposer of that portion of the universe which comes under our observation, but, in some measure, as he is out of that portion, they connect us with the scheme of his invisible providence, with God as he is the Father of spirits, rather than as a temporal guide.

Whilst, however, each vehicle of knowledge to man has its appropriate end, each is in a secondary manner subservient to the end of the other. A knowledge of our spiritual condition must powerfully conduce to unfold to us the advantages attached to our present condition of being, by giving us the true moral of our circumstances in those enlarged views of the divine administration which it developes; and thus a scriptural revelation must promote the temporal happiness of man. So, on the other hand, nature must lead us to our spiritual good, at the same time that she ministers to our temporal wants; as a discernment of the truths of natural providence is identified with an acquaintance with God. For whether we "eat or drink, or whatsoever we do, we do all to the glory of God." We do not indeed glorify Him with our hearts, unless we perceive with our hearts that connexion which the natural blessings of life have with His sustaining hand, and thus convert our enjoyment into an act of obedient piety: but still, whilst we follow the plain directions of nature, in order to our temporal good, we tacitly confess the wisdom and goodness of that arrangement of things to which we conform ourselves.

If this be a correct view of the different kinds of good primarily intended under the two different modes of divine instruction, it will follow, that the scriptures will reveal in larger profusion and with more extended reach of thought, the riches of the sacred treasury of wisdom. We must hear of God in them, not simply as He is cognizable to us, when we are necessarily occupied more immediately in learning that knowledge of Him which terminates in the exigencies of our present life; but as He is a God who must be known in order to the invisible life of the soul.

As nature gives a more copious information respecting all things necessary for the life on earth, and is almost silent or obscure on things simply spiritual; so will a scriptural instruction, which *really* comes from God, leave the mere things of time in comparative darkness, whilst it dwells with particularity of detail on such subjects as are needful for the formation of the life of God in the soul of man. In the arts and sciences which contribute to the support, the comfort, and the ornament of life, nature, accordingly, is our perfect instructor; for all these have their end in this present world; and if we sought therefore for as full, or as correct, information concerning them in the pages of the scriptures, we should certainly be disappointed. But the scriptures, indifferent to truth or error on such matters, as not belonging to their province, invite our steps beyond the barriers of our present condition, and present to the uplifted eye of faith the mysteries of godliness. The ways of eternal life are the arts about which they are employed. Here then they are full and express. The principles of holy living are unfolded by them, as they are in truth; whilst the principles of all other arts are neglected. Thus even moral philosophy, so far as this science is simply conversant about our temporal relations, and capable of being viewed as distinct from religion, is left to the discovery of human reason *; whilst the enduring part of the science, the consideration of it, in its full extent and proper nature, as it is grounded in just views of the Divine character, —as it tends to the formation in us of that frame of mind which is requisite for the enjoyment of spiritual happiness †, and which will survive the

---

* "It is observable, when the Scriptures recommend chastity, temperance, justice, and mercy, they never give any definition of those virtues, but barely name them, supposing the world was acquainted with their nature, and that the observance of them, as well as the forbearance of the contrary vices, were the dictates of the light of reason, and the result of the moral nature of things." "Essay upon the Laws of Nature", by Sir Richard Blackmore.

† Aristotle indicates his conviction of the imperfection of that view of moral philosophy, which respects the temporal relations alone of mankind, where he insists on the necessity of cultivating the divine principle of our nature in that noble passage of his Ethics: Χρὴ δὲ οὐ κατὰ τοὺς παραινοῦντας, ἀνθρώπινα φρονεῖν, ἄνθρωπον ὄντα, οὐδὲ θνητὰ τὸν θνητόν· ἀλλ' ἐφ' ὅσον ἐνδέχεται ΑΠΑΘΑΝΑΤΙΖΕΙΝ, καὶ ἅπαντα ποιεῖν πρὸς τὸ ζῆν κατὰ τὸ κράτιστον τῶν ἐν αὐτῷ· εἰ γὰρ καὶ τῷ ὄγκῳ μικρόν ἐστι, δυνάμει καὶ τιμιότητι πολὺ μᾶλλον ὑπερέχει πάντων, Lib. X. c. 7. He mis-

temporary occasions by which it has been formed and disciplined,—is set forth with a height and a depth of philosophy with which no human wisdom can compete*.

Whilst, accordingly, the truths taught by the scriptures and by the natural world, must agree essentially in some common principles of the Divine administration, they must also differ actually as to the degree in which they evidence such principles. In investigating the philosophy of Christianity, we must ever bear in mind that

takes indeed the nature of the divine principle in man, not including in it a capacity of moral improvement, since he limits it to νοῦς, or intellect. Nor does he lay down any precepts in order to that immortalizing of our nature of which he speaks: but here he laboured under the want of a supernatural revelation, without which he could go no further than he did.

* To this refers the well-known remark of Josephus,—οὐ γὰρ μέρος τῆς ἀρετῆς ἐποίησε τὴν εὐσέβειαν, ἀλλὰ ταύτης τὰ μέρη τἄλλα συνεῖδε καὶ κατέστησε· λέγω δὲ τὴν δικαιοσύνην, τὴν καρτερίαν, τὴν σωφροσύνην, τὴν τῶν πολιτῶν πρὸς ἀλλήλους ἐν ἅπασι συμφωνίαν· ἅπασαι γὰρ αἱ πράξεις, καὶ διατριβαὶ, καὶ λόγοι πάντες, ἐπὶ τὴν πρὸς Θεὸν ἡμῖν εὐσέβειαν ἔχουσι τὴν ἀναφοράν· οὐδὲν γὰρ τούτων ἀνεξέταστον οὐδὲ ἀόριστον παρέλιπε. Contra Apionem, II. 16. Op. Tom. III. p. 1260, Oberthur.

we are reasoning from the works of God, *as he is our God*—the God who doeth wonders in the earth—to the invisible operations of the Lord God of Sabaoth;—from that comparatively little scheme of things of which we constitute the whole, to that scheme, ineffably amazing in its comprehensiveness, as including the created myriads of eternity, of which we constitute only a part. Whilst we justly apply therefore the principles acquired in the school of natural theology to the scriptural truths, we must give them a latitude coextensive with the vastness of the subjects to which they are transferred. The same principle, which in our own circumstances appears frustrate, and distorted, and imperfect, must expand itself into a perfect and unexceptionable law, when it passes from the narrow prison-house of the visible world, in which it is pent up and obstructed, into the boundless regions of the new heavens and the new earth.

> Largior hic campos æther et lumine vestit
> Purpureo, solemque suum, sua sidera norunt.

Here then, where all that now impedes must be

conceived to be done away,—what is begun of the scheme of Providence in this world shall obtain its completion,—what is partial shall become universal,—what is limited and circumscribed shall assume a vastness and indefiniteness of outline,—what is seen only in tendency shall be consummated in effect.

Hence appears the necessity of making allowances, in the application of our general observavations from the facts of experience to the doctrines of Scripture, for the circumstances under which they are made, as well as for those to which they are applied. We must not expect to find an exact coincidence in any instance, until we have abstracted from the truth, as collected from experience, all that is peculiar to experience, and from the truth revealed, all that is peculiar to the scriptural lessons of instruction.

Thus we must refer each to that state of things with which it is immediately connected. We must examine whether, when all those circumstances which may naturally be supposed to produce the observed difference in the actual developement of the theological truth, according as it belongs to the system of nature or that of grace, are taken into our consideration, the same abstract truth emerges as the point of ultimate coincidence. For if nothing appears to prevent such an ultimate coincidence of a fact of nature and a scriptural truth, but the peculiar circumstances of the two systems to which they respectively belong, it is evident that the two may justly be conceived as ultimately coinciding in principle, since they then appear as therefore only not coincident actually, because their circumstances are not.

Hence it is that the credibility derived to the scriptures from the coincidence of their doctrines and circumstances with the facts of nature, is that which belongs to the evidence of analogy. For by analogical reasoning we are enabled to make the requisite references to the circumstances by which a general truth may be variously modified, and to express the result of such references in our conclusion. When we argue by induction, the conclusion embraces all the circumstances belonging to the facts upon which our observations have been made. We reject and exclude all that are merely accidental, but we rigidly preserve in the general proposition every particular which appears really to belong to the effect produced. Whenever, therefore, any circumstance really important is varied, our former induction fails, and we must then either repeat the experiment, or if actual experiment be impracticable, we must have recourse to analogical reasoning; that is, to a mode of reasoning which affirms the conclusion with such reserves, such alterations, or exceptions, as may arise from any difference in the circumstances to which it is extended. Without indeed such a relative adaptation of the general truth as obtained by induction to the altered circumstances of the case, the inference would be evidently unsound, as appears from this consideration alone—that, as every induction is relative to the circumstances under which it is made, and as analogy is only a substitute for induction, so also must analogy express, or at least imply, that relation to the altered circumstances, which would have been expressed, had the conclusion been directly obtained by induction. And whether we are able to state exactly the effect which these new circumstances may produce, or can only allow for it by an implied reference to them, the conclusion is equally logical; since in either case we do not proceed beyond the limits of the premises *.

---

* A particular instance (or several instances) may be employed for the purpose of deducing either a general or a particular conclusion. In the first case we argue by induction, or conclude concerning the whole class to which the instances adduced belong: in the latter case we argue by analogy, or conclude concerning a different instance of the same class to which the instances adduced belong. Examples, which differ from instances in general only so far as they belong exclusively to the subject of human life, are employed for either purposes, and are accordingly either arguments by induction or by analogy, in respect of the conclusion deduced from them. If we conclude *generally* that some degree of civilization should precede the reception of Christianity from the example of any particular nation viewed at the time of its conversion to Christianity, we conclude by induction; but if we argue from the same example to the case of the Hindoos, or of any other people, we conclude by analogy.

The form of every analogical argument may be thus stated:

It remains, however, to ascertain, whether the allowances which we make for the peculiarities

Whatever belongs to this particular (or to these several particulars) belongs to any other particular of the same class.

This (some property inferred from observation) belongs to this particular.

Therefore the same property belongs to this other particular of the same class.

Or if we assume the same major premiss in each of the following cases, the minor and the conclusion might thus be stated.

A design of tyranny is what belongs to this instance of THE CLASS.

asking a body-guard. (Pisistratus at Athens, or Theagenes at Megara.)

Therefore such a design belongs to this other instance of THE SAME CLASS.

asking a body-guard. (Dionysius at Syracuse.) Arist. Rhet. p. 49. Buhle.

The quality of justice belongs to this instance of a THE CLASS.

moral effect produced (where a human agent is concerned).

Therefore the same quality belongs to this other instance of THE SAME CLASS.

the like moral effect produced (where a superhuman agent is concerned).

It appears, accordingly, that there are two requisites in

of each mode of divine instruction, in tracing out by analysis the common principles into which order to every analogical argument. 1st. That the two, or several particulars concerned in the argument, should be known to agree in some one point; for otherwise, they could not be referable to any one class, and there would consequently be no basis to the subsequent inference drawn in the conclusion. On this account it has been shewn at the outset of this inquiry, that nature and divine revelation must contain some common principles. 2dly. That the conclusion must be modified by a reference to the circumstances of the particular to which we argue. For herein consists the essential distinction between an analogical and an inductive argument. Since, in an inductive argument, we draw a general conclusion; we have no concern with the circumstantial peculiarity of individual instances, but simply with their abstract agreement. Whereas, on the contrary, in an analogical argument, we draw a particular conclusion, we must enter into a consideration of the circumstantial peculiarity of the individual instance, in order to exhibit the conclusion in that particular form which we would infer. Whence it follows, that, whilst by induction we obtain absolute conclusions, by analogy we can only arrive at *relative* conclusions, or such as depend for their absolute and entire validity on the coincidence of all the circumstances of the particular inferred with those of the particular from which the inference is drawn. Whence also it is, that analogy has been explained as meaning " not the similarity of two things,

they are ultimately resolvable, may be identified with those variations in the facts of each system,

but the similarity or sameness of two relations." (Dr. Copleston's " Enquiry into the Doctrines of Necessity and Predestination." Notes to Disc. III. p. 122.) For the two particulars which are rightly connected in an analogical argument appear only as coincident in one point—that in which they are represented in the premises as belonging to one class: any further coincidence is dependent on the coincidence of their circumstances; and their actual or formal resemblance, consequently, is only of a relative nature.

Analogy is sometimes stated as an argument from species to species. (Mr. Dugald Stewart's " Elements of the Philosophy of the Human Mind," Vol. II. Ch. IV. Sec. IV. p. 404, 8vo.) And it may justly be so considered, if we regard the analogous particulars as specific instances of the class to which they are referred, which then becomes their genus—and if we are careful to distinguish such a genus from any supposition of homogeneity in the *nature* of the particulars: since any agreement in an external point of view suffices for such a classification; or, otherwise, the application of analogical reasoning must be restricted to cases where we know beforehand that the particulars, about which it is sought to employ it, are of a kindred nature; a restriction which would render analogy comparatively useless as an instrument of discovery. The mistake to which this last observation refers, is akin to that which confounds the relative resemblance of the particulars connected

which might be anticipated in reasoning by analogy concerning the truths of Scripture, from

in an analogical argument, with their absolute, in supposing the latter to exist when only the former appears. Both errors proceed on the false principle, that analogy, as an instrument of investigation, gives us instruction respecting the intrinsic nature of the particulars which it connects, instead of its being, as it really is, only the means of classifying different subjects, so as to extend inferences from the known to the unknown. A human person, a picture, and a statue, are all analogous to each other, if they agree in presenting a certain expression to the outward observation. This uniformity of expression is independent of the different materials from which it results, and it is on the ground of its existence, under the diversity of materials, that we pronounce them to be likenesses of one another.

There are some valuable remarks on analogy in Dr. Hey's "Lectures in Divinity", Vol. I. p. 162. That excellent writer's account of analogy, however, is defective; as he does not point out the effect of a *difference* in the circumstances to which we reason, in modifying the inference. He contents himself with stating, that " when circumstances are changed, our analogy how strong soever, instantly *vanishes*"; whereas it should rather have been observed, that the analogy then assumed another form. He asserts also, that " conclusions by analogy are not properly reasoning"; which is not true. If we refer to the *observations* on which an analogy is founded, we might then

the data furnished by experience. For this is necessary, in order to shew that the facts of nature, and doctrines of any particular revelation, such as that of the Scriptures, are really analogous to each other. If the difference between a scriptural truth and its counterpart in the system of nature, were greater or less than such as might be attributed to the difference of circumstances, the scriptural truth could not in such a case be regarded as a *conclusion* from experience. Nor could the Christian Religion be established as philosophically true.

The validity of every analogy being dependent entirely on the accuracy with which the relation to the peculiar circumstances of the case is consulted in the conclusion, it is important to our purpose to point out, by some examples, the various ways in which the effect of these circum-

say, it was not " properly reasoning", but in the act of stating the analogy a process of reasoning is involved, and the conclusion is a logical deduction from premises, as is shewn above. (See Dr. Whately's Chapter on Induction, " Elements of Logic ", p. 207.)

stances may be stated, or implied, in a conclusion deduced by analogy.

The circumstances to which we reason may be considered of threefold character. They are either known, or unknown. If they are known, they are; —1. Either such as we have no reason to think different in any respect from those under which our observations have been made; or 2. Such as differ in certain *known* respects from these last. 3. They are unknown, where we reason concerning truths of which, from the state of our present knowledge, from the nature of our faculties, or from the accident of our situation as sojourners upon earth, we are totally ignorant. Accordingly as the circumstances of the case belong to one or the other of these three classes, the conclusion deduced by analogy is variously modified.

1. When we reason from the past to the future, we infer an event exactly similar to that which has preceded, because we constantly suppose a continuance of the same circumstances as those under which our observations have been made. Thus when we presume on the daily rising of the sun, we conclude with reference

to ourselves, by whom the observation of his past rising has been made; that is to persons situated as we are on the globe. We see no reason that any circumstance essential to the fact should be varied on the morrow or on any following day, and therefore we conclude that the fact will recur in the same form. But though we have no reason to suppose that there will be any variation, yet it is impossible for us to rely on a future event with the same confidence as on the past; we know not whether something may not intervene to disappoint our expectations; whether there may not be some error in the supposition of an exact similarity of the cases so brought together; and analogy here requires us to qualify the conclusion with that imperfection which necessarily attends on all human anticipations. So also when we speculate on the future conduct of individuals or bodies of men, it is always the supposition of the known similarity of the circumstances which justifies the similarity of the event inferred; whether we argue concerning the same individual and the same bodies of men, or from one individual to

F

another and one society to another. The only modification introduced here by analogy is, as before, such as belongs to the contingency of the future compared with the certainty of the past.—To the same class of analogies may also be referred those instances, in which we beforehand exclude from our consideration certain known differences in the circumstances of two subjects, and determine to draw an inference from one to the other only concerning one point in which they are supposed to agree, our argument not being affected by their disagreement in other respects. For example—colonization was beneficial to Holland and Spain as maritime powers; therefore it will be beneficial to another country considered merely as such a power. The whole effect of colonization on the several countries would require to be exhibited very differently, if the question were whether it were generally expedient for another country to send out colonies after their example; but if we were considering simply the improvement of the marine of a particular state, we should need only to look to the effect produced in that one point of view. Or,—if Paganism, as an established religion, promoted social order and happiness, so will Christianity, *as such*, promote the same,—is an argument of the like kind. We studiously disregard the known differences, and our conclusion is valid, as far as it extends, without any reference to them. Still, as the cases connected in such arguments are really distinct in themselves *, and that exact and entire coincidence, which is necessary to justify us in regarding each as a substitute for the other, is a point assumed, the conclusion, though indisputably true as to all practical purposes, yet, in speculation, cannot be held as absolutely true in itself †.

2. When we know some definite particulars in which the circumstances to which we argue

---

* See Dr. Whately's " Elements of Logic", Chap. V. of the Dissertation on the Province of Reasoning, p. 264—269, and the Appendix; article, " same".

† Such analogies are the foundations of arguments à fortiori; such as, " If ye then, being evil, know how to give good gifts unto your children, how much more shall your Father which is in heaven give good things to them that ask Him?"

differ from those of the fact observed, the conclusion is then stated with that variation with which the known difference enables us to characterize it. Thus, if we would apply our observation concerning the rising of the sun to an inhabitant of the polar regions, we introduce the consideration of the known difference of latitude into the conclusion, and infer the periodical return of the sun at the interval of six months, as the correspondent fact, in the altered circumstances of the case, to that of his daily return in our latitude.—When the Puritans argued that the sacrament of the Lord's supper ought not to be administered to each communicant separately, because sermons are delivered to a whole congregation collectively; and that the communicants ought to sit at the Lord's table, because sitting is the proper posture at a supper: their argument in both cases was illogical, as the conclusion was not modified by the known difference of circumstances. As to the argument respecting the sacrament, an individual reception is here analogous to a collective reception of the benefits of preaching, because by an individual reception of it, the nature of the sacrament, or the peculiarity of the case, is respected; the sacrament being by its nature a *specific* application of the benefits of Christ's death, in contradistinction to sermons, which from their nature can only be a *general* application of the same benefits. " Equal principles", as Hooker observes in touching on this point, " do then avail unto equal conclusions, when the matter whereunto we apply them is equal, and not else."* The matter being here not equal, the conclusion required to be varied by a corresponding inequality. As to the argument respecting the posture at the Lord's table; kneeling here is analogous to sitting at any common supper; because we must take into consideration wherein the Lord's table differs from every other, and consequently unite adoration with feasting. When, again, the Papists argue the necessity of an infallible living judge in religious controversy, from the fact of a judge being employed as an expounder of human laws; the pretended ana-

* " Ecclesiastical Polity ", V. 68. p. 343, 8vo.

logy fails; because the different nature of religious truth, as compared with legal truth, is entirely overlooked in the inference. If we consider this difference, the conscience occupies that place in regard to religious truth, which the living judge occupies in regard to human laws; the conscience being the authority constituted by God as the ultimate interpreter of His laws, as the living judge is the authority constituted by the framers of human laws.—Again, the analogy between the different fine arts consists in the modifications which they exhibit of the principles of taste common to all, according to the materials employed by them in producing their effect. Hence we account for the absence of the eye in the sculptured form, whilst in a picture it is the life and soul of expression.—And thus Aristotle speaks of rhetoric as the *counterpart* of logic (ἀντίστροφος); it agrees with logic, in having no definite subject about which it is conversant; but the peculiar rules of the two differ as much as the subject-matter of an argument differs from its *form*.—Again, on the supposition of a future life, the birth and death of man are analogous events; by each event we are introduced into a new life; and the different nature of the future life, as an invisible state, is strictly respected in the difference of the event of death, as compared with the event of birth. Lastly, those analogies which run through different languages, and those which are the foundation of metaphor, may be adduced as instances of conclusions *expressly* modified by known differences of circumstances. Thus, in translating from one language to another, the same thought is retained by an idiomatic variation of expression, and not by an exact rendering of word by word. And when we apply the terms, *wing* and *oar*, metaphorically, each term expresses *that* in its own circumstances which the other stands for in its circumstances. The *wing* is to the bird in the air what the *oar* is to the vessel in the water*.

---

* Metaphors, so far as they are founded on correct analogies, have the nature both of arguments and of philosophical truths: for the justness of the analogy is that which constitutes the excellence of the metaphor; and wherever there is a just analogy there is a conclusion rightly drawn from premises,

3. We come to the consideration of those cases of analogy in which, from our ignorance of the circumstances to which we argue, we are unable to state in the conclusion those modifications which arise from them. These are cases in which we are most liable to fallacies in reasoning by analogy, because the justness of the argument depends on the *tacit* reference which is made by the mind to such qualifications of the fact inferred, as may be suggested by a consideration of our ignorance. If this implied

as well as a detection of a point of agreement in different subjects, which is the work of philosophy. Their actual futility as arguments, or deficiency in information as philosophical truths, does not affect their *nature* in either of these points of view. These circumstances depend on the *nature of the observations* from which the analogical inference is drawn. If these are unimportant the conclusion will be unimportant. That metaphors, and arguments founded on analogy, differ only as to the points to which our observation is directed, is shewn by the Provost of Oriel, in his admirable dissertation on Analogy, p. 125, of his " Enquiry into the Doctrines of Necessity and Predestination ", and his " Remarks upon the Objections made to certain Passages " in that Enquiry, p. 37.

reference be not made in our estimate of the force of the conclusion, the argument is illogical. Thus if the celebrated illustration of the Athanasian Creed, in which it is said that, "as the reasonable soul and flesh is one man, so God and man is one Christ", were understood to convey a notion that the union of the two natures in Christ was exactly the same kind of union as that of a human soul and human body—the real force of the illustration would be altogether destroyed. If, on the other hand, we recollect that we are arguing to a case whose circumstances are past our comprehension, and retract our assertion, as it were, at the same time that we advance it, within the limits of our knowledge; we shall understand it as meaning, that there is some kind of inconceivable union of two distinct natures in the person of Christ, as there is some kind of inconceivable union of two distinct natures in the person of a man. Of the kind of union we venture not to pronounce, but we suppose it to be as different from the fact adduced in illustration of it, as its relation to an unknown

Being may render it; and *therefore* the analogy is justly asserted. Again, our Lord's illustrations of the powerful and secret agency of the Holy Spirit by the invisible power of the wind, and of the benefits of His death by the corruption of "a corn of wheat" in order to its vegetation, would be greatly perverted, unless the indications from experience were qualified by a reserve of the judgment in their analogical application. We must guard against supposing, that the operation of the Spirit is represented to us in its mode, by the invisible force of the wind; or that the process of vegetation at all adumbrates the work of redemption; and remember, that the two conclusions only hold good when the mysteriousness of the subjects about which they are conversant, is also strictly maintained in them. Again, the beautiful allusion made by Addison *

---

* " With what astonishment and veneration may we look into our own souls, where there are such hidden stores of virtue and knowledge, such inexhausted sources of perfection! We know not yet what we shall be, nor will it ever enter into the heart of man to conceive the glory that will be always in reserve for him. The soul, considered with its Creator, is like

to " one of those mathematical lines that may draw nearer to another for all eternity, without a possibility of touching it", in illustration of the endless approach of the soul of man to the perfections of its Creator, can only be regarded as a very faint presumption of the fact; as the difference of circumstances is infinite between a mathematical fact, the subjects of which derive their nature from the definition of them, and are therefore precisely ascertained, and a physical

one of those mathematical lines that may draw nearer to another for all eternity, without a possibility of touching it: and can there be a thought so transporting, as to consider ourselves in these perpetual approaches to Him, who is not only the standard of perfection, but of happiness?" Spectator, No. 111.

To the mathematician it is some drawback from the pleasure which this illustration excites to know, that the fact, though mathematically true, is not physically so; and that even mathematically considered, the asymptote approaches so near to the curve as to be ultimately a tangent: for his mind will revolt from the idea, that the created being, however sublime in moral and intellectual perfections, can ever so closely approximate to the Creator. The general reader will not perceive this objection, and will therefore have a greater relish for the illustration.

fact, conversant about subjects whereof our knowledge is scanty and obscure. All that it shews is, that the two ideas of, an infinite approximation, and an infinite distance, of two objects, are not inconsistent in one case, and therefore may not be in another; but the particular case adduced is so extraordinary, that the analogy almost vanishes.

This last species of modification is that which belongs to all speculations on the subjects of religion. We may judge indeed, to a certain extent, of the variation in the form of a general principle, when that principle is transferred to the circumstances belonging to a scriptural truth, so far as the exclusion of the *finite* may help us in framing a just conclusion. Apart however, from direct information from God concerning the things of that His larger invisible kingdom, wherein is comprehended that portion of it which is open to our observation, we know nothing positively of the circumstances to which we reason; and we must, therefore, make ample allowances for the real ignorance and incompetence under which we labour, in all our attempts to explore these untracked regions of divine providence; and be careful that we admit nothing into our reasonings which would imply our experimental acquaintance with them.

But, from the same cause, we are also bound to admit any information concerning them, which comes within the pale of our ignorance, and which at the same time is authenticated to us by adequate testimony, as an ingredient in the conclusions deduced by analogy. For it is the due consideration of our ignorance which renders the conclusion valid in the former case, and it is only a result of the same consideration that, in the latter case, we actually qualify the observations of experience with any particulars communicated to us by express message from God.

Any particulars, accordingly, which the scriptures reveal, purely belonging to the unknown invisible world, may be regarded as identified with those variations of the fact observed in nature, which we should argue, by just analogy, independently of the scriptural information.

These revealed particulars, in fact, only enable us to make more exact statements in the analogical conclusion, of the weight which our ignorance ought to have in the argument. They are amongst those reserves, exceptions, or alterations, with which the truth, as learned from experience, must be *understood* by us in our uninformed state; and therefore exist in the conclusion, by implication, antecedently to the views unfolded by the scriptures.

Any new form consequently which a law of nature may assume, consistently with the scriptural views of the invisible world, (it being presumed that the scriptures have their proper evidences of authenticity as records of truths purporting to be delivered by persons specially sent from God,) is a valid extension of the induction from experience. It is valid, as being an adherence in our conclusion to the confession of our natural ignorance, which we are obliged to make at the outset of our investigation.

To make it appear, then, that the doctrines of Christianity are instances of truths relative to the invisible world, capable of being regarded as just conclusions in the way of analogy from the data of experience, it will be useful to refer to some particulars in which its correspondence with experience is discernible.

First, let us compare the doctrine of a future life, as it is scripturally revealed, with its counterpart, as it is made known to us by the course of the world.

The scriptural doctrine of a future life coincides with the facts of nature in the two following general principles or laws of the divine administration.

1. " That all things will continue as we experience they are, in all respects, except those in which we have some reason to think they will be altered :"—2. "that the same creatures, the same individuals, should exist in degrees of life and perception, with capacities of action, of enjoyment and suffering, in one period of their being, greatly different from those appointed them in another period of it." *

* Butler's Analogy, Part I. Chap. I.

The first of these laws is evidenced in every thing that we observe around us, and is accordingly adopted by us as an indisputable axiom of conduct. The philosopher assumes it as a certain truth, when he lays it down as one of the laws of motion, that a body at rest will continue at rest, or if in motion will continue in motion; and the common man tacitly acknowledges his conviction of it, whether he commits his seed to the ground in the hope of a future harvest, or trusts in the known veracity and honesty of another person, or anticipates reward or punishment to himself at some future occasion for his past actions.

The second law is evidenced to us in the various instances which present themselves of the same animals passing through different conditions of being—emerging from the worm, or the shell, to the winged state; in the transitions of man himself from the womb to infancy, from infancy to mature age.

Now the scriptural doctrine of a future life coincides with the facts of nature in these two general principles; because it implies that we shall preserve our personal identity after death, that is, that we shall continue the same active and percipient beings in a state after death (or in a " posthumous life ", as Butler terms it), that we were before death; death having no power to destroy us as active and percipient beings; and because, again, it implies that we shall undergo a change in order to qualify us for our future existence, since " flesh and blood cannot inherit the kingdom of God." So far then as the scriptural doctrine includes these two notions respecting a future life, so far it may be stated as exactly coincident with the teaching of experience.

But the scriptures further tell us that the state of being on which we enter after death is imperishable and unalterable; or rather, that it is our final condition, there being no other appointed to succeed it; and, in regard to the modification which our nature will receive, they add that we shall rise again with our bodies, and that our bodies will then be spiritualized; and, as to our whole nature, that it will be purified, rendered like that of angels, and become susceptible of a happiness utterly beyond our present capacities of enjoyment.—Are these additions, we may inquire, such as may correctly be admitted into our conclusion, in arguing to the doctrine of a future life merely from the data of experience? This is the same thing as to inquire, whether those general laws of the divine administration, already adduced as points of coincidence between the scriptural doctrine of a future life and the facts of nature, being regarded simply as conclusions from experience, and extended by analogy to the larger scheme of God's invisible providence, would lead us to expect a future life such as that revealed to us in the scriptures.

Now to establish this point it is evidently not necessary that they should actually present the same views of a future life which the scriptures unfold;—it is only necessary that they should *tend* towards the scriptural views; since, from the considerations previously suggested, the lessons of experience must naturally be supposed inferior in distinctness and perfection of knowledge to the wisdom which descends more immediately from above. An approximation to the full truth in the former method of instruction, is equivalent to the full truth itself in the latter.

If we consider then our future existence in a state of perception and action, as a truth inferred by analogical application of the above-mentioned conclusions from the facts of nature to the circumstances of the invisible world, we shall find that, in allowing for our natural ignorance of the peculiar case respected in the argument, we should argue to a truth like that of the scriptures. For whilst experience teaches us to expect a continuation of our life after death under some different modification of being, yet if we look to experience alone without the requisite allowances for our ignorance in this case, we should infer a continuation of life under successive varieties of condition and forms of being, rather than that single, permanent, and invariable state, of which the scriptures discourse to us;—since the argument for a future life, derived from those changes which we perceive the same individuals undergoing and yet retaining their identity, in itself as much proves a succession of different future states, as it proves that there is another state beyond the present. Thus, the Pythagorean metempsychosis may be considered, in this respect, a literal adoption of the teaching of experience. Or when the Platonist, the Romanist, and the Socinian, assert the existence of a purgatory, they may be said to adopt a notion in exact conformity with those facts of nature which evidence the law of successive variations of condition appointed to the same individual creatures. But still the argument derived from those facts, for either the Pythagorean or Platonic doctrine, is fallacious, for the conclusion does not embrace the circumstances involved in the premises. The very exactness of the conformity, where we cannot know how great the difference of circumstances may be, shews that we have only *copied* servilely from the book of nature, and not *reasoned* from the data placed in our hands. For if we reason from them as we ought, we shall forbear to assert positively, in the absence of any express information from God on the subject, any thing respecting the *nature* of that future existence to which the facts of experience point. It is enough for us to argue, that our life will be continued through and beyond our death. Our being possessed of our faculties of perception and action up to the moment of our death, and our having survived through other modes of existence, shews demonstratively that we *may* live beyond death. But here we must stop. To proceed further, and to affirm, that when we die we pass into a particular state of being, or have a succession of different states appointed to us, is to omit entirely the requisite consideration of our ignorance concerning the circumstances of the case.—And the reason of the difference between our concluding from experience simply that we *may* exist hereafter, and concluding in this, or that way, respecting the *mode* of existence is; that, in the former conclusion, we take up nothing that may be regarded as peculiar to the facts of experience. We view them abstractedly, and thus obtain general principles, in which the facts of God's invisible providence may coincide under great actual diversity of form. But, on the other hand, when we conclude any thing concerning the *nature* or *mode* of our future existence, we multiply the necessary points of agreement so far, that it is no longer probable that the facts of the invisible world should coincide with them to such extent,—the supposition of such a coincidence being contrary to the presupposed possibility of an immense difference in the circumstances of the case to which we argue.—We are therefore open to receive any limitation or extension of our conclusions from mere experience, which a faithful messenger from God may suggest, by the knowledge which he imparts to us of a state after death. If he tells us accordingly that having once passed through the change from life to death, we shall die no more, but shall rise with spiritual bodies, and live for ever—a future state of such a kind is the real analogy to the course and constitution of the world. If we have argued correctly, independently of his information, we have held our conclusion from experience concerning the fact of our future existence, with that reserve which leaves us at liberty to superadd to it any detail of particulars which his gifted insight into the Divine ways may enable him to disclose to us.

Let us examine next that doctrine of the scriptures, which affirms, that "they that have done good shall go into life everlasting, and they that have done evil into everlasting fire"; and ascertain whether such a doctrine may be justly stated as analogous to the facts of nature.

1. First then it is to be observed, that nature presents indications of the truth of this doctrine, in those facts which concur in establishing the principle, " that the general method of Divine administration is, forewarning us, or giving us capacities to foresee, with more or less clearness, that if we act so and so, we shall have such enjoyments, if so and so, such sufferings; and giving us those enjoyments, and making us feel those sufferings, in consequence of our actions"[*]:—such as are, the evident instances, of the preservation of our lives depending on our use of sustenance—of advantages depending on our exertions to obtain them, and of evils arising from

[*] Butler's Analogy, Part I. Chap. II. p. 48.

our imprudence or neglect. This doctrine of religion accordingly, inasmuch as it implies a notion of God as a rewarder and punisher of men, has, in this respect, a point of coincidence with the facts of nature—being an instance of the same law of responsibility of man to God, which is evidenced in them.

2. Nature presents another point of coincidence with this doctrine in those facts which demonstrate, that it is a principle of the divine proceeding, that virtue should have the superiority over vice ; such as are—1st. Those instances already referred to, as illustrative of God's natural government over us ; for these are at the same time instances of one species of virtue, prudence, obtaining the advantage over one species of vice, imprudence. 2dly. Instances of the punishments and rewards which take place through the instrumentality of human governors. 3dly. Instances, in which a sense of merit or demerit in actions is felt to be a reward or punishment by an individual in his own mind, or actuates others towards him. 4thly. Instances, in which we perceive *accidental* hindrances to a more

righteous distribution of rewards and punishments than is actually discerned. The scriptural doctrine, accordingly, as implying the final triumph of virtue over vice, is an instance of that natural superiority which it appears to possess in the course of the world.

3. Another general principle in which this doctrine coincides with the teaching of nature is, that God has put our happiness and misery in a great measure in our own power. This is a law of the divine proceeding, deducible from the same facts which declare God's natural government over us. For all those instances which shew the necessity of our acting with a view to the consequences of our actions, in order to obtain the advantages and avoid the evils of life, shew also, by necessary implication, that our happiness and misery are appointed to depend, in part, at least, upon ourselves.

4. Again, this doctrine of religion involves another principle of the divine proceeding;—that God does not *at once* place us in that condition of happiness or misery for which we are ultimately intended, but *disciplines* us before-

hand by a preparatory state of being, which is our *opportunity* for securing the one, and avoiding the other. If we further interrogate nature on this point, we shall find her unanimous in proclaiming the same principle. For we find that we are not ushered at once into the duties of mature life, without a preliminary training during the period of youth, wherein we gradually and insensibly acquire the rules of conduct; and experience indeed in general shews us, that, whilst we are naturally unqualified for any particular station or employment, we are endued with capacities of acquiring and forming a character in ourselves, which we had not before; and that a certain character, accordingly, is the *result* of a previous discipline of habits leading towards it. So that the fact, that our whole ultimate condition of happiness or misery should be appointed to follow as a *consequence* of our conduct during a preparatory state of being, is an instance of God's dealing with us in regard to the scheme of His invisible providence, as He has evidently dealt with us in the course of His visible administration.

We have before us, accordingly, several points of coincidence between the scriptural doctrine of a final retribution and the course of nature. We proceed to inquire, as in the former case with regard to a future life, whether these general laws of the divine proceeding which constitute the points of coincidence, supposing them to be conclusions from experience alone, would suggest to us a religious truth, capable of being identified with the doctrine of the Scriptures.

From having learned then by experience, that God exercises a government over us in this world; that this government is moral, dispensing reward to virtue, and punishment to vice; that He has put our happiness and misery in our own power, so far that our respective portion of either is in a great measure dependent on our conduct; and that He disciplines us by a preparatory course of action for performing our part well in the various situations of life;—what are we to conclude respecting the circumstances over which His invisible providence extends?

We are only warranted then in concluding by analogy, that God will continue hereafter to exercise that government over us which He now does (or that He will hereafter render us obnoxious to the foreseen consequences of present actions) in a far more perfect manner, consistently with the enlarged scope of operation which His government obtains in the world beyond our view : that hereafter virtue shall be triumphant, and vice shall be finally depressed; for such a conclusion is the just consummation, under the invisible kingdom of God, of those beginnings of a righteous administration, and those impeded tendencies of virtue, which are discerned on the narrow scale of His worldly providence : that the happiness which is now hazarded on our conduct, shall hereafter be obtained by us, or lost beyond recovery; for what is *now* trial, difficulty, and danger, when referred to the invisible world, becomes *trial completed,* or peace and security on the one hand, and trouble and perdition on the other : that as we are now undergoing a moral discipline, we must be destined for a higher condition of virtue and happiness in the invisible world; since what is now *opportunity* of moral improvement, if we take into our view a larger scheme of Providence beyond what actually appears, points to a period hereafter, as the *crisis* of qualification, or disqualification, for that, for which the opportunity has been vouchsafed. Any one of these analogical inferences gives us ground to look forward to happiness or misery at some period after this present life; and all, taken together, excite a very forcible expectation that it will ultimately, " on the whole, be well with the righteous, and ill with the wicked "*.

But the state of retribution unfolded by the scriptures, gives us a much greater insight into the method by which the ways of God shall be justified hereafter. They acquaint us that a distribution of rewards and punishments, rendering to all their dues, shall take place by the sentence of a final judgment; when " the dead, small and great," shall " stand before God," and be "judged out of those things which are written in the books according to their works ":

---

* See Butler's Analogy, Chap. II. III. IV. and V.

that the reward of the righteous shall consist in their seeing God, and the punishment of the wicked in their exclusion from His presence: that both soul and body shall participate in the alternative of reward or punishment: and that the happiness or misery hereafter appointed to us shall be without interruption and without end.

Now all these particulars, it must be acknowledged, are matter of express revelation from God. They are peculiar modifications of the general fact of retribution, arising from the peculiar circumstances of another state of things, with which we are totally unacquainted by nature, and whose effect accordingly in varying the conclusion as obtained from experience, we must learn by direct information. The signs of nature can lead us no further than to expect that every man shall receive at some future day, and in some more perfect manner, of the fruits of his virtue, or the wages of his iniquity,—they are misconstrued and perverted, when they are made the basis of any hypothesis concerning the time or the manner in which this retribution shall be accomplished*. If we so apply them, we cease to *reason* from them (as was observed with regard to the indications of a future life); forgetting that our conclusion is only valid, when we understand it with that reserve which our real ignorance of the nature of the case demands.

If we suppose then these particulars imparted by the scriptures concerning a state of retribution, to rest on their proper evidence of authenticity, as parts of a divine message, we are bound to accept them as legitimate modifications of the inference from experience. And the doctrine accordingly, in its full scriptural acceptation, is the true analogy to the course and constitution of nature.

So we might proceed with respect to other doctrines. It might be shewn that the doctrine

---

* Here then we may again see the illogical ground on which the doctrine of purgatory in the absence of all scriptural sanction rests, as well as the fallacy of the notion held by some Arian Presbyterians, of a temporary punishment of the wicked to be terminated by annihilation.

of the fall of man from a state of original perfection, is analogous to that constitution of the natural world, which exhibits the operation of corruption even among the most perfect productions of nature*,—the operation of corrup-

---

* No fact appears to have been more strongly impressed on the minds of heathen writers than that of the degeneracy of the world. We perceive it in Homer's allusion to a race of men better than those οἷοι νῦν βροτοί εἰσι, and in the melancholy tone of his poetry throughout. So in Herodotus we find Solon observing to Crœsus, that " man is entirely calamity", " that it is better for him to die than to live." (Clio. 31, 32.) Thucydides attributes to Pericles the sentiment that " it is the nature of all things to degenerate"; (II. 64.) and in the speech of Diodotus, where he repeats the sentiment more pointedly (III. 45.) he supposes a better state of things in the early ages, when punishments were lighter: and Aristotle in accounting for the cautiousness and despondency of old men, ascribes it to their experience of the imperfection of human things, observing that " most things are bad ", that " many things turn out for the worse", and he remarks " a degeneracy in the families of men similar to that of the productions of the soil." (Rhet. II. 13 and 15.).

From an observed *tendency* in natural things to corruption, we certainly could not correctly argue to *a similar tendency* in such a being as man, any more than from the fading of the

tion as distinct from a *tendency* towards it; since the question then only is, whether the actual deterioration of a nature perfect in its kind is incredible, when there are visible instances of such deterioration in many of the works of God: or that the doctrine of man's future restoration to happiness through the sacrifice of Christ offered once for all, is analogous to those facts which shew in general that men are appointed to depend in some measure on the instrumentality and cooperation of each other, in obtaining not only the advantages but the common blessings of the present life; or to such as shew that bad consequences, which must inevitably have

leaf we could argue to the decay of the living principle in our bodies:—in order to argue such a tendency in the moral and intellectual nature of man, we require an instance of such a tendency in some other moral and intellectual nature. The fact, however, that a corruption *exists* in human nature is all that the scriptures assert; and this is rendered credible by parallel instances of corruption in other works of the Almighty hand. So far are the scriptures from asserting any *necessary* tendency to corruption as belonging to a moral being, that they imply the *contrary* in the account they give of angels who kept their first estate of good.

H

followed as far as our own ability to avert them is concerned, have been often averted through painful exertions voluntarily undergone by others: or that the doctrine of the secret influence of the Spirit is analogous to those mighty effects which we observe produced in nature by invisible agencies; or to those instances which evidence a tacit conviction of the Divine presence in the heart of man; when, for example, a feeling of horror takes possession of the mind at the thought of entire destitution and abandonment to itself,—that feeling so affectingly portrayed in the agony of our Saviour on the cross, when he cried out, "My God, my God, why hast Thou forsaken me!"—which Cain reckoned as a punishment greater than he could bear—and which perhaps in every case is the principal bitter ingredient in the cup of remorse*, the iron entering into the soul of the criminal apostate.

---

* It is beautifully depicted in the story of Bellerophon;

"Ἀλλ' ὅτε δὴ κἀκεῖνος ἀπήχθετο πᾶσι θεοῖσιν,
Ἤτοι ὁ καππεδίον τὸ Ἀλήϊον οἶος ἀλᾶτο,
Ὃν θυμὸν κατέδων πάτον ἀνθρώπων ἀλεείνων."

Iliad. Z. 200.

Or, if we look to the circumstantial character of our scriptural instructions, (since it is in this point of view that a comparison is open between Christianity and nature, as well as in the doctrines themselves,) here also we may detect just analogies.

Take that circumstance belonging to the scriptural truths, their connexion and mutual relation to each other in one scheme :—since it is evident that all have a reference to one end, the salvation of man by a Divine Person, the Messiah; and from their reference to this one end necessarily results their combination in that mode to which we give the name of a scheme or constitution. It is not their logical connexion which is here meant, or their implication of each other, as when we deduce the doctrine of a future life from that of a present state of trial and discipline; for this suffices merely for the purpose of forming human schemes of theology, or systematic arrangements of scriptural doctrines. But it is the simple union of those truths, as they have been brought together by the Divine Mind—as they tend, by mysterious ties of brotherhood with each other, to renovate the faded image of God in the soul of man, and to make him one with Christ even as the Father and Christ are one—which we now consider; and in respect of which we would trace a correspondence in our instructions by nature.

Now the facts of the natural world are evidently combined in a vast scheme or constitution, and a constitution of the like kind to that which we observe in scriptural truths; inasmuch as the only account we can give of it is, that the facts are so connected with each other as to tend to one common result, without our being able to discern the whole scope of that connexion or its necessary links. We can distinctly perceive, that it is a general fact of the divine proceeding in the world; that events are not absolute and independent of each other, but that by their " reciprocal correspondences and mutual relations, every thing which we see in nature is actually brought about."* Upon the general estimate, all the events of nature appear, as far

---

* Butler's Analogy, p. 173.

as we can trace them, to have some reference to the natural good of man. Part of this reference is the wonderful connexion observable between physical and moral causes[*], both thus constituting one great natural system, in which means are progressively carried on for the melioration of the condition of man in the world. Or if we look to more particular instances, we find parts of this great system in themselves composing minor systems in conformity to the plan of the whole—in like manner as each planet in itself, then the planets with their satellites in the solar system, and the solar system amidst the hosts of the constellated universe. For instance, that a man should act on some occasion in a particular way is dependent on his character, and the opportunity, or some casual influence which has prevailed over his ordinary judgment,—his character has been formed by his previous habits,

[*] As the improved cultivation of the soil, and abundance of the necessaries of life, resulting from improved civilization and knowledge in a country; and, vice versa:—the effects of climate and great national visitations, such as wars and pestilences, as modes of discipline to the moral character of a people.

those previous habits by his early education and associates; and so on: each circumstance in the inquiry leading us to some other connected with it, until, in the process of exploring, we lose ourselves in a labyrinth of antecedents and consequences.

From this principle thus illustrated in nature, we might argue, that if God should impart to us any knowledge of the facts of His invisible providence by a special revelation, the truths so communicated would, in like manner, be reciprocally connected with each other, and tend to some general result. But the kind of connexion to which we should thus argue analogically, may be as different from that observed in nature, as the different circumstances of the theological truths may cause them to be. Here in the world, events appear to arise out of one another according to uniform laws, and in the way of antecedents and consequences, and we see often their immediate subserviency as means by which some particular end has been attained. But there may be no such apparent connexion in the facts of the invisible world of Providence; the laws of their connexion may be entirely beyond our powers of perception; where the notion of time vanishes, the succession of antecedents and consequences also vanishes; and the means by which the several particulars contribute to their common end, may appear disproportioned and desultory; or there may be something fundamentally wrong in our very notion of them as *means* and *ends* *. The connexion of them may be simply revealed to us without our being able to discern it: as for instance, the connexion between the work of the Holy Spirit in the heart and the sacrifice of the Son of God in order to the salvation of man†; or the relation of each fact separately considered to that end; whilst we are left in ignorance as to the mode of connexion or relationship. So that, whether the scriptures explain to us more or less of that constitution or scheme of truths which they announce, the state of mystery in which they may leave the

---

* See Butler's Analogy, Part II. ch. iv. p. 267.

† "It is expedient for you that I go away; for if I go not away, the Comforter will not come unto you; but if I depart, I will send him unto you." John, xvi. 7.

subject, is what may justly be conceived to arise from the peculiar case of those truths; and that constitution which belongs to the scriptural doctrines may be regarded as the proper counterpart of that which belongs to the facts of nature.

Take again another principle of the divine procedure involved in the circumstantial character of the scriptural truths; that important facts are made known to us, repugnant to the anticipations of speculative reason; and that we are required to believe them without having been endued with capacities or principles for judging of them a priori*. Let us examine, therefore, whether nature does not lead us to suppose that, in the event of a supernatural revelation being vouchsafed to us, the truths so imparted would be greatly different from the anticipations of reason, or such as we might

* Butler's Analogy, Part II. ch. III. The term *anticipation* seems more properly to denote opinions founded on assumed principles, and *expectation* to denote such as are founded on analogies. Bacon applies *anticipatio mentis* to the old philosophy, as distinguished from his, which is *interpretatio naturæ*.

fancy liable to great objections, if we judged of them otherwise than by the analogy of nature. It is of consequence to observe, that expectations founded on the analogy of nature are not to be confounded here with the opinions of speculative reason, for to such expectations legitimately deduced from clear facts, it is impossible that an authentic scriptural revelation can be really repugnant, however it may appear so on a superficial survey; so that no objections against well-authenticated doctrines can ever be founded on real analogies; whereas mere assumed principles must be pregnant with strong objections against such doctrines, for this very reason, that they are assumed. But *the fact* that such principles do fail us in nature, is what we are now examining.

Is it not apparent then that facts present themselves to our observation, under the natural providence of God, repugnant to the anticipations of speculative reason? Consider the instances—of our knowledge of comparative distances from the joint operation of the senses of sight and touch—of single vision with two eyes—of our perception of erect objects from objects represented invertedly on the retina of the eye—of the power of the will over the limbs of the body—of the knowledge which brutes obtain, by means of instincts and propensities, and that acquired by mankind, by these together with reason [*], considered either separately or in comparison with each other—of the dispensation of gifts in general, and in particular of knowledge and talents, out of that order in which they appear most important to us or most properly bestowed; as in the earlier advancement of the science of astronomy compared with that of medicine, and the union of great talents with immorality in some individuals—of the diffusion of knowledge being made to depend on so imperfect an instrument as language—of improvements in arts resulting from so capricious a thing as sudden invention—of late discovery of important remedies of diseases, and their uncertain and imperfect operation when known—and numberless other instances which must readily occur to every thoughtful person—and the fact must be acknowledged, that many of the

[*] Butler's Analogy, Part II. ch. III.

phenomena of the natural world are such as are greatly repugnant to principles by which we might endeavour to judge of them a priori, and are really objectionable therefore when we view them by the light of these principles. For might we not argue, that it is impossible that the senses of sight and touch could be so conjoined as to produce a common result; that from a twofold representation of objects, a twofold vision must be produced; and from an inverted picture of an object, a perception of the object inverted; that it is absurd to suppose that thought could have any influence on the body, since its nature is such that it cannot act on matter; that instinct in brutes was incapable of producing those effects which we observe it produce in informing and preserving them; or of at once effecting in them, in some instances, what in the case of mankind is only gradually learned with the additional aid of reason, or what mankind with reason superadded cannot accomplish at all, or not so perfectly; that from our notions both of the wisdom and goodness of God, and of the subjects which would naturally first solicit the attention of mankind, it must follow that sciences most important to the preservation of human life would precede in the order of discovery—that great talents and great knowledge must always be united with great moral worth—that God would more effectually provide for the communication of knowledge than to leave it to the uncertainty of human language—that He would take care that every discovery important to man should be made by regular process of inquiry, and known early—and that the remedies to diseases should never fail?

If then we follow nature as our guide, we may well calculate on finding many scriptural truths very different from the anticipations of speculative reason. If, however, the sceptic further insists, that the irreconcileableness of scriptural doctrines with certain principles is still stronger than that which is apparent between the like principles and facts of experience—that it extends to more particulars—or that they are not merely irreconcileable, but disagreeable and unwelcome, exacting a self-denial of the intellect which would receive them, as well as of the heart which would embrace them;—we may reply, that the analogy which we assert between nature and scripture is not violated, but established by this very peculiarity. It is that which renders the analogy just and valid in this point. For that the case of the scriptural truths should exhibit greater eccentricity from the orbit which reason would mark out for them, and that they should more peremptorily disclaim to be measured by the rules of arbitrary hypotheses, is what may reasonably be attributed to the illimitable regions in which they expatiate, wherein we vainly attempt to track them, "as a ship that passeth over the waves of the water, which when it is gone by, the trace thereof cannot be found, neither the pathway of the keel in the waves."

But as Christianity is not a simple revelation grafted immediately upon the instruction of nature; but, so far as it is a particular religion, was preceded by the Patriarchal and Jewish dispensations, whilst, in that sense in which it comprehends them all, it is the one only true religion of the world; it will more fully illustrate the point here insisted on, viz.—that any two consecutive revelations of divine truth will be connected in the *way of analogy*,—if we extend our survey to some points of coincidence between Christianity and the elder associated revelations.

God has manifested himself as the same Lord, by exhibiting evidences of the same laws of divine administration under all three dispensations; but we may observe, that the forms which those laws assume, or the points of view to which the faith of mankind is peculiarly directed, are characterized by the circumstances belonging to the religion in each case.

What the extent of the knowledge of divine things, possessed by our first parents in their Paradisiacal state, was, we their degenerate descendants can form no satisfactory conjecture. Possibly, when the image of God was as yet unsullied in man, when all the principles of our nature were in their due proportions, and natural and moral effects were perfectly coincident, that fulness of light concerning the ways of God, which it required a succession of inspired messengers, and a period of four thousand years, afterwards to introduce to the world, was shed abroad at once upon their hearts, and they were enabled to worship God in the spirit and truth of Christianity. Our estimate, however, of the Patriarchal religion must commence from that state in which it was modified by the fall of man, when the heart and the intellect of the disobedient children of God were disturbed from their original rectitude, and had unlearned those hymns of praise which the diviner revelations of Eden may have inspired. Man then appeared first in that relation in which he stands towards God as a *suppliant for pardon;* and, thenceforward, the measure of the revelation vouchsafed was regulated by the occasions presented in the course of the world, for a disclosure of the counsels of God in regard to the grant of that pardon. Then began that special display of the Divine Being as a *gracious* God, which terminated in the incarnation and death of Jesus Christ, and the consequent effusion of the Spirit, in the latter days; when the full truth concerning the designs of God towards man was expanded, and the concentrated light of all the various manifestations of His will revealed the Trinity in Unity*.

Now the truths concerning God which would be suitable to the earliest revelations, are such as relate to the self-existence, spirituality, unity, power, wisdom, and goodness of God. These are the grand truths upon which all more intimate knowledge of the Deity must be founded. The knowledge of the mystery of the Trinity evidently presupposes them as known, since it is an addition of the notion of personality to

---

* Eusebius is fond of representing the Patriarchal religion as Christian in its institution and mode of holy living. Τοιοῦτος δὲ πέφηνεν ὁ πρὸς τοῦ Σωτῆρος ἡμῶν Ἰησοῦ Χριστοῦ νενομοθετημένος νόμος τε καὶ βίος, τὴν παλαιοτάτην καὶ πρεσβυτέραν Μωσέως εὐσέβειαν ἀνανεούμενος, καθ᾽ ἣν ὁ θεοφιλὴς Ἀβραὰμ, καὶ οἱ τούτου προπάτορες δείκνυνται πεπολιτευμένοι. Εἰγοῦν ἐθελήσειας τόν τε Χριστιανῶν βίον, καὶ τὴν ὑπὸ τοῦ Χριστοῦ πᾶσιν ἔθνεσι καταβεβλημένην θεοσέβειαν συνεξετάσαι τῷ τρόπῳ τῶν ἀμφὶ τὸν Ἀβραὰμ ἐπ᾽ εὐσεβείᾳ καὶ δικαιοσύνῃ μεμαρτυρημένων, ἕνα καὶ τὸν αὐτὸν εὑρήσεις. Euseb. Dem. Evang. Lib. I. cap. v. p. 9. He is fundamentally correct in this statement, but he does not make sufficient allowance for the distance of time at which the Patriarchs lived under a scheme of religion gradual in its developement.

what we naturally conceive to be the essential discriminative character of Divinity. And not only are they required as the ground-work of a higher theology, and therefore proper at the commencement of the scheme of divine interpositions, but the deficiency of natural instruction concerning God from the want of experience in the beginning of the world, indicates the need of express revelation on these points at such a period, and consequently their appropriateness as the themes of the Patriarchal religion. To enforce these truths, accordingly,—the sanctification of the seventh day,—the expulsion of our first parents from Paradise,—the denunciation of woe on the murderer Cain,—the translation of the righteous Enoch,—the preparation of the ark,—the flood,—the re-appearance of the dry land after the flood, and continuance of the order of nature,—the prohibition of eating blood, with the accompanying declaration of divine vengeance on the manslayer,—the confusion of tongues at Babel, and consequent dispersion of mankind,—the call of Abraham,—the destruction of the cities of the plain, with the rescue of Lot from the general overthrow; and the pillar of salt, that standing memorial of the necessity of immediate, unhesitating, unreserved obedience to the divine commands,—the commuted sacrifice of Isaac,—and all the various emergences in which God appeared counselling and helping the appointed instruments of His mercy to mankind,—were especially directed.

But though the character of God was thus principally developed to the Patriarchs in such particulars as belong to the fundamental notion of Him, and illustrate more especially the providence of nature; still there were some indications also of that sublimer knowledge of Him which results from a survey of the providence of grace. Whatever of compassion, whatever of forbearance, whatever of love, appeared in the primeval revelations,—from that it might have been inferred, that there was an invisible scheme begun, in which some more recondite truths concerning God were involved. These imperfect signs, viewed in connexion with the express promises of one who should " bruise the serpent's head", and of a blessing which should extend to " all the families of the earth", were the faint outlines of those mysteries which were afterwards declared in the events of the gospel. They are such approximations to the doctrines ultimately revealed in the Christian dispensation, as may be justly attributed to the simple and elementary nature of the Patriarchal religion; and are therefore, so far as they are discerned, instances of an analogy subsisting between the two systems.

Had mankind advanced in moral and intellectual improvement proportionably to the divine instruction with which they were favoured, it might have been expected that God would have lifted up the light of His countenance upon them with continually increasing brightness, and the stream of revelation would at once have widened more and more as it proceeded in its course. But the fact is otherwise. In vain had the earth been purified by the waters of the deluge. Apostasy had desolated its regions with the overflowings of ungodliness, and swept down all the landmarks of ancient piety and wisdom. It became necessary, consequently, to renew, and to redeliver in a more striking and palpable manner, those very truths which had already been promulgated to the world in the first revelation. Instead of an enlargement of the knowledge vouchsafed to the Patriarchs, we find accordingly the following revelation immediately conversant about the facts of natural providence, and busied in retracing the obliterated vestiges of its predecessor. And, as in the outward aspect of the world at the time of its delivery, it was a difficult, if not an impossible, task to discriminate, amidst the moral chaos, between the apparent course of things, and their real order as proceeding from the hand of God, a revelation was needed, which should point as it were with its finger to the agency of God, and command the attention of the world. Such, we observe, was the character of Judaism. It exhibited a restoration of that union between natural and moral good, and between natural and moral evil, which the corruption of the world had entirely obscured, and presented clear and indubitable phenomena from which a true notion of the Deity might be obtained.

From the peculiar circumstances, accordingly, in which the Jewish revelation was vouchsafed, resulted that peculiar form which theological truth assumed in it. It expressly repeated, indeed, the principles of the Patriarchal religion, for it embodied them in its records as connected with its own origin; but, so far as it was a new and distinct revelation, it modified them by a reference to its immediate end; the reestablishment of the visibility of Divine Providence. So also it continued to expand the designs of God towards mankind beyond the horizon of the Patriarchal religion, and to usher in the dayspring from on high; but with a subdued tone, and an immersion of its rays in the shadows, which its connexion with a temporary purpose threw around it. In both cases, all truths concerning the Deity were represented in subordination to that of a particular superintending Providence.

Thus, the unity of God is inculcated throughout the Jewish revelation, as well in strong express declaration, as by the tenour of the narrative; but if we look to the first commandment, in which the truth is stated as it peculiarly belonged to Judaism, we find it proclaimed, not in the terms which belong to universal religion, but as connected with the display of a special Providence. It was the Lord who brought the Israelite forth out of the land of Egypt and out of the house of bondage, besides whom he was forbidden to have any other God. So, again, when the observation of the sabbath is enjoined; though in the fourth commandment it is grounded on an universal principle—the rest of God after the work of creation—the duty is afterwards placed on the peculiar ground of Judaism*. In relation to the peculiarity of the religion, may be interpreted also that account of

---

* "And remember that thou wast a servant in the land of Egypt, and that the Lord thy God brought thee out thence through a mighty hand, and by a stretched out arm; therefore the Lord thy God commanded thee to keep the sabbath day." Deuteronomy, v. 15.

See Mede's Works, Vol. I. p. 74, folio, 1664.

the character of God, which it presents in describing Him as a *jealous* God, visiting the iniquities of the fathers upon the children; as well as that peculiar view of His moral government which it exhibits in the exact dispensation of temporal rewards and punishments. If we inquire what account Judaism gives of the appointment of a Mediator, we again find the nature of the religion checking the full developement of the doctrine, and overlaying the sacred truth with temporal promises and ceremonial observances connected with the peculiar institution*. The doctrine of a future life, in like manner, was but faintly and obscurely intimated under that system; sufficiently indeed to kindle the hopes

---

* " Behold, I send an angel before thee, to keep thee in the way, and to bring thee into the place which I have prepared. Beware of him, and obey his voice, provoke him not; for he will not pardon your transgressions: for my name is in him. But if thou shalt indeed obey his voice, and do all that I speak; then I will be an enemy unto thine enemies, and an adversary unto thine adversaries. For mine angel shall go before thee, and bring thee in unto the Amorites, and the Hittites, and the Perizzites, and the Canaanites, the Hivites, and the Jebusites: and I will cut them off." Exodus, xxiii. 20—23.

of the devout believer, though not as an express object of his faith; whilst, on the contrary, length of days on earth, and continued possession of the land of their fathers, were held out to the Children of Israel as the proper inducements to obedience*.

It would however too much interrupt the direct course of the present inquiry, to touch on these points with that distinctness and fulness of illustration, which both their importance and their interest demand†. It is enough for our

---

* " And Moses made an end of speaking all these words to all Israel: and he said unto them; set your hearts unto all the words which I testify among you this day, which ye shall command your children to observe to do, all the words of this law. For it is not a vain thing for you; because it is your life: and through this thing ye shall prolong your days in the land, whither ye go over Jordan to possess it."—Deuteronomy, xxxii. 45-47. This passage is particularly cited, among a great many others to the same purport, from its emphatic force as the conclusion of the recapitulation of the law.

† It belongs also to this subject to point out how the successive revelations during the Patriarchal age of religion; as well as those of Judaism considered as including, not only the dispensation of the law of Moses, but the subsequent interpositions during the continuance of that law; were modified by

purpose, to see that other revelations, whose truth is implied in the truth of Christianity, *may be shewn* to correspond with it in the way of analogy; and reverting accordingly to the position, that Christianity and the instruction of experience exhibit proper correspondences in their respective systems, we next inquire what is the degree of evidence resulting from such an agreement.

The nature of the credibility, obtained to the scripture revelation from its agreement with the voice of experience, being then the correspondence of analogous facts in the two systems of divine instruction,—we shall readily estimate, from this account of its nature, the force with

the occasions, as far as our knowledge of them extends. But such a discussion would lead us into a very wide field of inquiry. The Discourses on Prophecy of Mr. Davison may be referred to, as affording ample evidence of the fact. By the masterly view presented in that work, of the progress of the prophetic light, we are enabled distinctly to trace the Divine wisdom adapting its successive partial communications to the condition of man, until, as Mr. Davison beautifully expresses it, prophecy " expired with the gospel upon its tongue."

which the evidence of the natural world acts as a means of substantiating the truth revealed.

Now, every analogy implying a coincidence only in some general principle common to the different facts which it compares together, it follows, that where by virtue of such a coincidence the existence of one of the analogous facts is argued from the known existence of the other, there is always more inferred than is actually warranted by experience. The fact so inferred accordingly, whilst the analogy is justly asserted, may at the same time not be true, or, in other words, amounts only to a *presumption*.

Analogous facts, when employed in argument, may be compared to two witnesses agreeing in some one point of their evidence, of whom one is known to be worthy of credit, but the other is either altogether unknown or less known. We can only then be sure that the unknown, or less known, witness has spoken truth, as to that single point; but at the same time, the coincidence of his testimony on this point is a strong ground for believing his evidence to the whole extent.—So, the doctrine of an atoning

Saviour agrees in evidence with those particular facts of experience, which shew that vicarious punishment is a law of the Divine administration in the present world:—this general truth is the point of evidence in which such facts and the scripture doctrine agree;—so far then we may be sure that the doctrine in question has spoken the truth; not only *verisimile,* but *verum:*—but finding it actually true thus far, we have ground for believing the whole complex notion of an atonement in its scriptural acceptation; the whole taken together is, *as if* it were true, or *verisimile.*

Now, if two witnesses were capable of attesting the same truth *throughout,* and still only agreed in one point; such a coincidence, so far from being a ground of belief to either, would throw discredit at least on one of the two. But if, on the contrary, their circumstances are such, that no coincidence could be expected but in that single point in which they do agree; then is this limited coincidence a stronger ground of inference to the belief of the less known witness than if they had agreed further.—This is precisely the case with the conspiring evidence of two analogous facts. They cannot be supposed to agree beyond a certain point;—they can only *generally* agree; because some difference between them is always, either known, or supposed possible. The difference between the whole evidence contained in the unknown fact, and the known fact with which it partially agrees, is such as is conceived to result from the peculiarity of the subject; and this consideration, accordingly, renders such difference more credible than a more perfect agreement would be in such a case.—The doctrine of the Atonement evidences the general principle of vicarious punishment; but the addition to this evidence made by the scriptural intimation,—that Christ has once for all atoned, by his death and sufferings, for the sins of the whole world,—is only such a variation from the evidence to the same point given by the facts of experience, as the different circumstances of the scriptural truth may naturally impose,—and it is therefore *in its subject* more credible than a more complete agreement would have been.

The credibility thus obtained to any doctrine

of scripture, is capable of being increased in two different ways : either by the simple repetition of analogous instances in the course of nature, all illustrative of the same general principle : or by the variety of instances in which, as compared with one another, *different* general principles are contained; each of them however coinciding in some point with the religious truth.

The doctrine of a future life, for example, as we have seen, may be argued simply from those facts of nature, which agree in shewing, that existence of the same individuals, under different modifications of being, at different periods, is a general law of nature; and, the more frequently that such facts have occurred to our observation, the stronger, of course, is the evidence to the law itself, and consequently to the doctrine in which it is involved. Or we may appeal to another class of observations from which we infer, that it is a law of nature, that existence once begun is continued, where there is no sufficient impediment to such continuance; and a future life, being also coincident with these observations in this point, is further confirmed by a various and independent evidence.

On the other hand, the credibility of any doctrine from analogy, may be diminished by instances apparently illustrative of the contradictory of some principle implied in that doctrine. For example, the improveableness of man by habits,—a general fact, taught by experience and implied in the scripture doctrine of Retribution,—may appear to be contradicted by those instances which shew that improvement beyond a certain degree is not attainable in our present condition; as when the strength of an individual is overwrought, or the powers of the mind are exhausted by too intense exercise. Such instances constitute exceptions to the general observation founded on those which indicate the constant improveableness of our nature: and the analogy consequently to the doctrine of scripture is to be estimated with allowances for such militant instances. If the last should preponderate in the scale, the analogy would be altogether destroyed.

The credibility, however, derived to Christianity as a *whole*, from its analogy to the course and constitution of the world, is to be estimated, not only by the coincidence of its particular truths with particular facts of nature, but from the combined weight of such coincidences considered as illustrative of the general theory of the religion so revealed. For any religion, abstractedly viewed, may be stated in the form of a general theory * by which the phenomena of the moral world may be solved; and under this point of view, each analogy of nature in which we behold a counterpart of any particular doctrine, is an evidence of the general credibility of the theory deduced from a collective survey of all the doctrines. And the religion, consequently, as a whole, though some of its doctrines may not be discerned in their analogy to facts of the natural world, is capable of being confirmed by the test of experience. As it appears indeed, that in each truth of revelation which has its counterpart in nature, there is more than is actually verified by the corresponding matter of fact, and that this excess obtains a credibility

* See p. 99.

from its being only such an enlargement of the truth experienced as may be required from the nature of the subject to which we transfer it: so it may be argued, that even such truths of the Christian revelation, as, while they are not contradicted by experience, do not appear to have any counterparts in nature, are yet rendered perfectly credible by means of the observed correspondences in other truths belonging to it; and from the same reason, that they may be regarded as an *excess* of information attributable to the peculiar subject.

For though it is necessary, that there should be some evident agreement between the truths natural and revealed; it is not necessary, that this agreement should hold in every particular point *. It is only necessary that there should

---

* " For there is no presumption at all from analogy, that the *whole* course of things, or divine government, naturally unknown to us, and *every thing* in it, is like to any thing in that which is known; and therefore no peculiar presumption against any thing in the former, upon account of its being unlike to any thing in the latter. And in the constitution and natural government of the world, as well as in the moral go-

be no contradiction in any one point. And an agreement may still subsist in many points in which we have not yet discovered it.

At the same time it clearly follows that, the more numerous are the particular analogies, the greater is the force of the general analogy resulting from the fuller induction of facts; not only from the mere accession of particulars; but from the additional strength which each particular derives by being surveyed jointly with other particulars, as one among the correlative parts of a system. All the doctrines of scripture being associated, either by their reference to a common

---

vernment of it, we see things in a great measure unlike one another; and therefore ought not to wonder at such unlikeness between things visible and invisible." Butler's Analogy, Part II. Chap. II.

Hence even the apparent unlikeness of a scriptural fact to the course of nature, amidst a general conformity of their respective truths, might be argued to be a presumption in its favour; according to that topic of probability which Aristotle has expressed in these lines of Agatho:

Τάχ' ἄν τις εἰκὸς αὐτὸ τοῦτ' εἶναι λέγοι,
Βροτοῖσι πολλὰ τυγχάνειν οὐκ εἰκότα.

Rhetoric. II. Cap. XXIV. p. 296. Buhle.

end, or by their implication of each other; it follows that an evidence to the truth of any one is in some degree an evidence to the rest.—Presumptions, for instance, of the doctrine of the Atonement are indirect presumptions of other doctrines,—such as, the efficacy of prayer, and the influence of the Holy Spirit,—not *intrinsically* connected with each other to our apprehension,—yet bearing on the same end,—the final salvation of man. Again, a future state implies the moral government of God; or the moral government of God implies a future state—trial and moral discipline are also included in the notion of moral government—and so on, as to other doctrines. Analogies, consequently, pointing out the probability of a future state, are indirect illustrations of the truth of any of these other doctrines, with which it appears to be so intimately connected.—Christianity indeed, to be rightly appreciated, in its evidence, no less than in its interpretation, must ever be regarded as a religion coherent in all its various parts, and entirely harmonious with itself. This admirable coherence, this divine harmony, observable throughout it, is in itself a powerful argument of its truth; but it is of peculiar importance in the comparison of the religion with the course of experience; for it is in consequence of it, that any single proof from matter of fact is increased an hundred-fold, by the multiplied lights reflected from every other link of the chain of evidence.

III. But this leads us to the consideration of another division of our inquiry—the Importance of the credibility thus derived to a scriptural revelation.

I. And first, under this head, its argumentative force demands to be considered:—or how far a supernatural revelation thus correspondent with the experienced course of nature, may be speculatively concluded to be divine in its origin.

It is evident, agreeably to what has been already stated *, that the argument now under our review, can only be demonstratively conclusive on the *negative* side.—Where, instead of cor-

* Page 11.

respondences with the course of nature, real discrepancies were perceivable in any assumed revelation, there we might positively decide that the pretensions to inspiration are false; and that the miraculous evidence, presumed as the basis of the whole inquiry into the truth of the revelation in question, in reality never occurred. The wisdom with which it professes to enlighten us, is not the same kind of wisdom with that which we have already known as divine; and therefore we cannot believe that the divine power could have been associated with principles so discordant.

On the other hand it must be conceded, that a revelation may exhibit many points of coincidence with experience, and at the same time be false. Indeed, without some conformity with experience, it seems impossible that any religion could obtain even a temporary currency in the world. A system of unmixed absurdity, which recoiled from all contact with the reality of human life, would carry too palpable a refutation of itself on its own front, to be received and embraced to any extent among mankind.

There might be some fanatical devotees to whom the very extravagance and unreality would be the strongest lure to its reception; but if we survey mankind extensively, the laws of nature will be found to exert their paramount ascendancy, so far as not to admit of an entire detrusion from their throne, though in some degree they may seem to compromise their right, and admit unworthy compeers within their proper dominions. Thus we find, even in those superstitions which are most revolting to common sense, some countervailing truths, which have both softened and recommended the associated mass of error, otherwise too grossly repulsive for the heart of man ever to have admitted.

But the application of the argument is at once reduced into the narrowest compass, by stating that it is altogether irrelevant, where any assumed revelation, to which it may be attempted to apply it, does not rest on the primary evidence of miracles. It is an accidental confirmation from nature of that which is essentially established by miracles.

The power of God being premised in a given revelation, it *then* becomes a question; what signs there may be in it of a wisdom and a goodness, such as may correctly be associated with this presupposed attribute: but, without this preliminary characteristic of divinity, there is no antecedent presumption that any revelation has been made, and no call for the comparison of the pretended revelation with the unwritten truths of nature. Mahometanism accordingly contains many truths which are part of a real revelation; since they have been adopted into that system of imposture from the authentic page of the Bible. Mahometanism, so far then as it contains such truths, symbolizes with the teaching of nature; and may seem therefore to have the evidence of the voice of nature in its favour: but these coincidences amount to no proof of the reality of the inspiration of the Koran; since Mahomet made no pretension to the power of working miracles. What is *professedly* established by man, can never be argued *subsequently* to be more than human. The internal marks of truth may be copied from some previous true revelation; when the external, that which appeals to the eye and ear, cannot be pretended to *have occurred*, in the absence of all proof, or pretension of proof, at the outset*.

* Mahomet evidently felt the want of miraculous power to secure a reception to his pretended revelations as divine; and hence propagated the belief that he was an illiterate person, calling himself "the illiterate Prophet": that the Koran might thus be a standing miracle in itself. A passage cited from the Koran (chap. xxix.) by Dr. White in his Bampton Lectures (p. 203, note) to this effect, is: "Thou couldest not read any book before this; neither couldest thou write it with thy right hand: for then had the gainsayers justly doubted of the divine original thereof." This mode of miraculous pretence was perhaps suggested to him by that passage of St. John; "And the Jews marvelled, saying, how knoweth this man letters, having never learned?" Chap. vii. 15. It is remarkable however, as a point of contrast, that Jesus does not take to himself personally, as Mahomet did, from this circumstance, any merit of the doctrine which he taught. Instead of taking advantage of the impression produced by his doctrine, so as to insist on the intervention of miraculous power in that particular respect, he calls upon the Jews in his answer, to practise what he taught in order to judge of the divinity of his doctrine:—for the internal proof of its divinity he sends them to their own hearts; for the external, properly so called, to the external works which he had wrought in their sight.

Further:—the confirmation of revealed truth from its analogy to nature, will depend on the importance, and extent, and variety, of the correspondences which hold between the two classes of facts. It will not be enough, that a conformity should appear only in a few points, or that the points of agreement should be of secondary importance. The confirmation must be strong and extended.

It is also material to observe, that whilst an agreement holds between the doctrines of a revelation and the facts of nature—the differences which they present must, in order to a just analogy, be no other than such as are referable to the peculiar circumstances of the invisible world. This consideration at once shews the futility of the Mahometan doctrine of a future state;—since, though as an intimation of our existence after death, it essentially agrees with the facts of nature no less than the Christian doctrine; yet the additions introduced into the general truth, are evidently the borrowed colouring of the scenes of oriental life*, and do

* This is only one absurdity of the Mahometan future

not leave the subject in that state of indefiniteness, in which, as a revelation of a great mystery, it must ever be left to the mind of man, whilst he is an inhabitant of this lower world, even though illumined with knowledge from above. There is a want of *keeping* in that picture of a future state; a distinctness of outline which brings the objects out of their proper distance. Possibly indeed, (for let us beware of saying that the Father of lights is limited as to the degree of wisdom which He may impart to our present faculties,) we may have been instructed as to many other particulars of a future life beyond those contained in the scriptures; and yet the state of our knowledge concerning it may have remained in perfect consistency with the teaching of experience*. It must only be observed

state. In another point of view it is a wide deviation from the established course of providence, by exhibiting happiness in connexion with sensual gratification, and not as the consequence of virtue. On this account it is irreconcileable with the principle of God's natural government.

* " And as the works of God and his scheme of government are above our capacities thoroughly to comprehend, so there possibly may be reasons which originally made it fit

that the particulars added by Mahometanism no longer permit us to regard the doctrine of a future life, in its Mahometan form, as *analogous* to the course of the natural world.

1. To come then to the particular application of the argument to a written revelation, such as that of Christianity substantiated by miracles. How forcible the confirmation to the truth revealed is in such a case, will appear, from contrasting the two forms of instruction which are thus brought to bear on the same points. On

that many things should be concealed from us, which we have perhaps natural capacities of understanding; many things concerning the designs, methods, and ends of Providence in the government of the world. There is no manner of absurdity in supposing a veil on purpose drawn over some scenes of infinite power, wisdom, and goodness, the sight of which might some way or other strike us too strongly; or that better ends are designed and served by their being concealed, than could be by their being exposed to our knowledge. The Almighty may cast clouds and darkness round about Him, for reasons and purposes of which we have not the least glimpse or conception." Butler's Sermon " Upon the Ignorance of Man."—Works, Vol. II. p. 266.

one side, we have a voice not of the world, proclaiming the truth taught, to be divine—on the other, we have the voice of nature, answering as it were to the challenge, and confirming the previous annunciation from heaven. We find two communications from the Deity to man, totally distinct in form, and yet closely agreeing in substance—the one, made known to us by the experienced course of the world in which we live—the other, accredited by an infringement of that course, and yet addressing us by the established signs of human intercourse.—This is a confirmation of a much stronger kind, than that derived to the theories of common sciences, from their correspondence with the facts which are the subjects of them. In all such cases nature furnishes the principles, and nature presents the tests of their truth. But when we have the truths of religion before us, written by the finger of God's special messengers, and altogether unconnected in their *origin* with the course of experience; the correspondence, which we then detect between them and the facts of the world, cannot but strike the minds of all who reflect on the different circumstances of the two things compared, as a very firm ground of conviction. The difference between the two forms of divine instruction must be conceded to be immense. The credibility consequently, obtained to the revelation from its analogy to nature, is strengthened, in proportion to the evident difficulty to mere human inventors, of nicely adjusting to each other, the results of such heterogeneous materials. It may be pronounced as morally impossible, if the assumed revelation were not really the authentic inditing of that Spirit which in the beginning animated the present order of the universe, that such a wonderful sympathy should be traced between its expressed dictates and the silent eloquence of nature. The experimental test to which the scriptures are thus submitted, would be too severe an ordeal for the pretensions of imposture. For what Bacon observes respecting experimental science in general, may well be transferred to the comparison between revealed religion and experience. " Quemadmodum enim in civilibus, ingenium cujusque, et occultus animi af-

fectuumque sensus, melius elicitur, cum quis in perturbatione ponitur, quam alias; simili modo, et occulta naturæ magis se produnt per vexationes artium, quam cum cursu suo meant."*
By resorting to such a comparison we view the truths revealed, altogether detached from their own sphere. We place them as in a situation of disturbance, where no hypocritical disguises can avail; and where a native unsophisticated strength of character alone can suffice for a triumphant display of their divine pretensions.

2. If, moreover, there be any thing in the internal character of the revelation in question which particularly invites to a comparison of this kind; if, instead of resting exclusively on its divine attestation, it call upon us to examine, whether it be of God, by the test which the actual occasions of human life afford; and is willing to stand or fall by the rigid criterion of experience: then we must acknowledge, that a discernment of its analogy to the course and constitution of

* Nov. Org. I. Aph. 98.

the world becomes most indispensable to the establishment of its truth; and by satisfying the adventurous claim of the revelation must place its credibility beyond all reasonable doubt.

Such then is the case with regard to Christianity. It expressly refers us to experimental proof of its divine origin; it directs us by the mouth of its great Agent and Interpreter, to "do the will" of God, if we would "know of the doctrine, whether it be of God"; by which precept, we may understand the necessity of examining the truth of that scheme of knowledge which it unfolds, by the test of its accordance with our nature and condition. For however this text of scripture* may be interpreted, as implying the necessity of a holy life in order to the right apprehension of the sacred truth; if we further consider the way in which a holy life thus contributes to the reception of Christian

* See the admirable sermon of Bishop Taylor on this text, entitled "Via Intelligentiæ".—Works, Vol. VI. p. 373. Also Archbishop Tillotson's series on the same. Vol. I. p. 235, folio.

doctrine, we shall trace it to an agreement between the right conduct of ourselves as rational beings, and the righteousness which is by faith; and such an agreement implies an identity of truth pervading both the systems of grace and nature.

3. But even if Christianity contained no such express intimation of its close connexion with the natural world, we should find ample authority for adopting this argument in the tenor of those instructions which it conveys. It is a revelation of practical utility. It is " profitable for doctrine, for reproof, for instruction in righteousness, that the man of God may be perfect, thoroughly furnished unto all good works." It holds out to us no expectation of that happiness, which it is its object to effect, from the mere intellectual possession of its heavenly stores of wisdom; but it sets forth that happiness as the *consequence* of acting up to the light vouchsafed—calling upon us to walk worthy of the vocation wherewith we are called; to work out our salvation; to make our calling and elec-

tion sure. On the whole, it exhibits the business of life, as immediately subordinate and instrumental to the bliss which it promises; not, like all false religions, leaving a wide chasm between this world and the next; but pointing out a connecting path, the narrow but sure way, which leads through the wilderness of the world to the land of promise: appointing the present state of being, as the field on which our moral strength must do valiantly, and on which the laurels of spiritual victory must be won, that the mansions of heaven may open their everlasting doors to our triumphant ingress in the train of the great Captain of Salvation. It evidently claims to be regarded, not only as the truth from above, but as a *saving* truth; not the light only, but the *life* of man. It therefore professedly adapts its information to the existing state of things. Having a direct subserviency to human conduct, it proclaims its glad tidings to us in a lively and energetic tone of practical exhortation.—But this practical character of the Christian revelation would be rendered altogether absurd, if the principles which it inculcated were such as were not echoed by the heart of man *. Accordingly, the very nature of Christianity directs us to seek proofs of its truth, by examining how far the actual constitution of ourselves has been respected in it; whether it exhibits a conformity to those active principles implanted in us by the Creator, which it is its express object to employ.

4. In subservience to this general observation on the practical nature of the Christian religion, it may be added, that it is a revelation which descends to particularities. It accompanies us, hand in hand, through the daily transactions of life, and mingles in social intercourse with us, as a companion and a guide, and a familiar friend. False revelations either presume, with bold cal-

---

* Τοῖς εἰσάγουσι κρίσιν δικαίαν Θεοῦ ἀποκέκλειστο ἂν ἡ ἐπὶ τοῖς ἁμαρτανομένοις δίκη, μὴ πάντων ἐχόντων κατὰ τὰς κοινὰς ἐννοίας πρόληψιν ὑγιῆ περὶ τοῦ ἠθικοῦ τόπου· διόπερ οὐδὲν θαυμαστὸν τὸν αὐτὸν Θεὸν, ἅπερ ἐδίδαξε διὰ τῶν προφητῶν καὶ τοῦ Σωτῆρος, ἐγκατεσπαρκέναι ταῖς ἁπάντων ἀνθρώπων ψυχαῖς, κ. τ. λ. Orig. con. Cels. I. p. 6.

Ὅρα δὲ εἰ μὴ τὰ τῆς πίστεως ἡμῶν, ταῖς κοιναῖς ἐννοίαις ἀρχῆθεν συναγορεύοντα, μετατίθησι τοὺς εὐγνωμόνως ἀκούοντας τῶν λεγομένων. Idem, Lib. III. p. 135. Ed. Spenc.

culation on the sequacious credulity of mankind, to transport us into scenes whose proper glories must ever be hidden from the inquisitive eye of man, so long as he dwells within the veil of mortality, or, with the lurking timidity of a conscious imposture, indulge only in general descriptions, which scarcely admit of any test of contradiction from the particular facts of our experience*. But where such pretended revelations are silent, or deliver their instructions only in a secondary tone of importance; there the more authentic shrine of Christianity delivers its oracles in clear and unambiguous and peremptory language. "This do, and thou shalt live," is the characteristic tone of all its sacred intimations. It never leaves us or forsakes us; but whether we " walk by the way, or when we lie down, and when we rise up," we still find our monitor by our side; ever prompting to some act of duty, however insignificant in the view of the world; or warning from some temptation to criminal excess, though the occasion be appa-

* Διὰ τὸ ὅλως ἔλαττον εἶναι ἁμάρτημα, διὰ τῶν γενῶν τοῦ πράγματος λέγουσιν οἱ μάντεις. Aristot. Rhet. III. C. v. p. 328. Buhle.

rently the most trivial. Like the luminary of the natural world, it sheds an irrespective illumination on little objects, as well as on the greatest; diffusing the animation and warmth of its moral lustre, amidst the lowliest, as well as the most splendid and joyous scenes—on the vales of human life, as well as on its high places,—on the quiet paths of private and domestic virtue, as well as on the ostentatious career of public exertion. Nothing is concealed from its searching eye—nothing is too mean to attract its vigilant superintendence.—A revelation, thus condescending to human wants in the minuteness of its application, must be continually exposed, if unfounded in the Divine wisdom, to receive a shock in some part of its system from the course of the world. Inasmuch as it professes to accommodate itself to the various emergencies of our earthly condition; its efficacy may be constantly called in question, by the numberless occasions which are momentarily arising in the current of human affairs, under every different form, to cope with it, and to try its strength and skill. It becomes therefore highly important, to examine, and disclose to view, its suitability to the circumstances of human life. It is important,—as well for the purpose of obviating imaginary objections, derived from any supposed incongruity in its system with the actual state of the world, by shewing how it aids, and conspires with, the natural and proper tendencies of worldly things to produce the good of man ;—as to illustrate that *individuality* of character which it claims to itself, as a revelation conversant about particulars, and admitting the utmost specific application to the occasions of life.

5. It should further be remarked, that Christianity is a revelation, which, far from offering its healing aid to mankind, as if it were endued with some mysterious charm,—producing instantaneous relief to the distempered soul, without any apparent connexion between the means employed and the result,—achieves its benevolent object of promoting human happiness, by the regulated instrumentality of human sentiments and actions. It presumes to disturb nothing, either in the mind of man, or in the

world, which is of natural appointment. It assumes all things to be good so far as they proceed from the same Divine Author, whom it claims as the inditer of its holy truths,—and it therefore affects not to undo, or dispense with, any thing which bears the real impress of his workmanship*. It aspires only to be the universal rule—to moderate and to conduct, towards its due perfection, that constitution of things which we find existing in nature. We learn from it, indeed, that the natural man cannot please God; and it insists on the necessity of an inward change by the work of the Spirit—regenerating us in the holy dews of baptism, and transforming us by the continued renewing of our minds—to render us meet for the inheritance of the saints in light:—but it is the natural man, as he is perverted by inbred corruption and by habitual sin—that adscititious temperament of soul now be-

---

* Gen. i. 31. "And God saw every thing that he had made; and, behold, it was very good."

Οὔτε γὰρ φύσιν φαύλην ὁ Θεὸς εἰργάσατο, οὐδέ γε ψυχῆς οὐσίαν· ἀγαθῷ γὰρ οὐδὲν πλὴν ἀγαθὰ δημιουργεῖν θέμις· ἀγαθὸν δὲ πᾶν ὅ, τι κατὰ φύσιν. Euseb. Præpar. Evang. Lib. VI. p. 250.

come our second nature—which Christianity requires to be changed; not the principles themselves given us, as it expressly alleges, after God's own image. The obliquity of these principles it would counteract—their unnatural distortions it would symmetrize—their defilements it would utterly cleanse: but, like the wise master builder repairing the dilapidations of some stately edifice— the remnant of the magnificence of other days—it discerns in the ruins the monuments of a venerable taste, and accomplishes its work of restoration by a faithful adherence to the original design of the fabric. As therefore it thus preserves in its system a scrupulous regard to the economy of the world—as it thus studiously designs to reform and improve, and not to reverse our nature—it may be regarded as tacitly acknowledging itself, by this its purport, amenable to the trial of its correspondence, with those principles of our nature, and those circumstances of our condition, which it assumes as the line of its operation, and as the points to which its scheme of moral improvement is directed.

6. Christianity again implicitly connects our present and our future happiness. It proclaims, that " godliness is profitable unto all things, having promise of the life which now is, and of that which is to come "*: a declara-

* " Seek ye first the kingdom of God and his righteousness, and all these things shall be added unto you." Matt. vi. 33.—" Verily I say unto you, there is no man that hath left house, or parents, or brethren, or wife, or children, for the kingdom of God's sake, who shall not receive manifold more in this present time, and in the world to come life everlasting." Luke xviii. 29, 30. Also Matt. xix. 29.

In the parallel passage of St. Mark x. 29, 30, there is an important addition in the latter clause of the sentence. It is there said, that the recompense in this world shall be accompanied " *with persecutions.*" If we connect this with what our Lord elsewhere says: " Think not that I am come to send peace on earth; I came not to send peace, but a sword," &c. Matt. x. 34. and " I am come to send fire on the earth ", Luke xii. 49, and with 2 Tim. iii. 12, " Yea, and all that will live godly in Christ Jesus shall suffer persecution":—we shall perceive with what limitations these accounts of the temporal prosperity of Christianity are to be understood; namely, that the happy temporal result, though flowing from the nature of the religion, will be produced so far as the circumstances of the world will admit of it. The counteracting tendency

tion, which must be construed as teaching, that the same institution of life under the Christian discipline, which carries us forward towards an eternity of bliss in heaven, enables us also to perform our part well on the transient stage of our existence in this world, and consequently to obtain all the peace, and satisfaction of mind, and real enjoyment, which the world is capable of affording amidst its manifold disorders and interruptions. It is not then the commencement of a new system of virtuous enjoyment which it proposes to us, but the perfecting of that which is already begun here on earth, however incomparable it may be in degree with the glory which shall be hereafter. It is *this corruptible*, in a spiritual, as well as a natural sense, which shall put on incorruption. It is *this mortal*, not only as to the grosser material part of our nature, but as to our capacities of virtue and happiness,

of the world must also be taken into our consideration, in order to obtain the actual external result. In the case of Judaism, the untoward circumstances of the world were overruled, and the temporal good effect of a true religion consequently took place invariably when that religion was obeyed.

which shall put on immortality. We learn, accordingly, from Christianity, to regard this present life as containing those germs of felicity, which shall grow up to their maturity, and blossom with unfading fruits, in the kindlier soil of the paradise of God. Now, therefore, if its system be founded in truth, must be discovered the efficacious working of those principles of religious belief and action, which are hereafter to obtain their full display and consummation: now must they be seen, at least, as in an adverse twilight, struggling with the surrounding darkness of the world, and faintly scattering their rays on the face of nature. Hence, we must resort to our experience, to examine what indications it possesses of the beneficial operation of Christian principles—to see whether those views of future happiness which our religion teaches us to adopt, have any real subserviency to the present state of things: whether they be not capable, in some degree at least, of acting with transforming power on the condition in which we are now placed, and of originating, however imperfectly, that happiness on earth, to which they point in the world beyond our view.

7. We may also argue the importance of the evidence from the analogy of nature to the Christian revelation, from the character of the instruction contained in the Bible.

It is easy to say that *theology* is the subject of the sacred volume; but under this term we may greatly misconceive the nature of the instruction which the Bible gives us. The theology which it teaches, is, as Bishop Taylor well expresses it, " a divine life, rather than a divine science ",—that is, it does not so much satisfy our curiosity concerning God, as it enables us to be conformed to Him in heart and conduct. The student in Christian theology is no inquirer into the nature of the Deity*. How far mere

---

* The nature of Christian theology is very happily described by Eusebius in the following passage. ... τίνες δ' ἡμεῖς, καὶ ὁποῖος ὁ τῶν τοιῶνδε λόγων τε καὶ μαθημάτων Διδάσκαλος, αὐτὸς ὁ Σωτὴρ καὶ Κύριος ἡμῶν Ἰησοῦς ὁ Χριστὸς τοῦ Θεοῦ, ὁ τὴν καινὴν ταύτην καὶ ΠΑΝΑΡΕΤΟΝ ΠΟΛΙΤΕΙΑΝ καθ' ὅλου τοῦ κόσμου συστησάμενος· ὥστε τοιαῦτα μανθάνειν, καὶ φιλοσοφεῖν, μὴ

information concerning God is from being the purpose of the scriptures, is sufficiently evident from the disappointment experienced by those who approach the study of them with the eye of the mere philosopher or critic; and the consequent errors of misbelief or infidelity, in which their sinister inquiry terminates. Whereas, had they looked upon the scriptures as a code of necessary information concerning the duty of man, they would have been led to perceive its clear adaptation to this end; and, admiring the marvellous light which it casts upon the whole condition of our being, have probably been induced, however reluctantly, to bestow an entire credit on that volume which so sagaciously unfolded to them the true moral of life *.

μόνον ἄνδρας, ἀλλὰ καὶ γυναῖκας, πλουσίους τε καὶ πένητας, καὶ δούλους ἅμα δεσπόταις. Demonst. Evang. Lib. I. Cap. vi. p. 24.

* Hence the declaration of Justin Martyr, who had been successively a Stoic, a Peripatetic, a Pythagorean, and a Platonist. After relating his accidental conversation with a venerable old stranger who had convinced him of the error of Platonism, he observes: Ἐμοῦ δὲ παραχρῆμα πῦρ ἐν τῇ ψυχῇ ἀνήφθη, καὶ ἔρως ἔχει με τῶν προφητῶν, καὶ τῶν ἀνδρῶν ἐκείνων οἵ εἰσι Χριστοῦ φίλοι· διαλογιζόμενός τε πρὸς ἐμαυτὸν τοὺς λόγους αὐτοῦ,

The Bible indeed, considered as an historical work, differs not from any other history as to its subject-matter. Man and his condition are the subject about which its narrative is conversant. But in this respect its history differs from all other histories, that it exhibits man and his condition, in those relations in which they stand towards God. Thus the origin of the world in which we are placed, as it came from the hands of God, and as it is a part of the universal creation, is expressly revealed to us:—thus the primeval state and the fall of man;—the fortunes of those individuals and of that nation, for whom, as the instruments of man's future restoration by a Redeemer, God especially interfered in the course of the world,—are prominently noticed and recorded as memorable

ταύτην μόνην εὑρισκον ΦΙΛΟΣΟΦΙΑΝ ΑΣΦΑΛΗ τε καὶ ΣΥΜΦΟΡΟΝ· οὕτως δὴ, καὶ διὰ ταῦτα, φιλόσοφος ἐγώ. Dialog. cum Tryph. Jud. p. 225, Op. 1686.

Daillé, in his work on the Fathers, p. 518, as quoted by Dr. Hey, Lec. in Div. Vol. I. p. 146, refers to this character of our scriptural instruction. " La sagesse exquise, et l'inestimable beauté, de la discipline même de Jesus Christ, est (je l'avoue) le plus fort, et le plus sûr argument de sa verité."

facts in the page of inspiration. And thus, in general, those circumstances of mankind at different periods of the world, which have, either in themselves or by their connexion with other events, presented striking occasions for the manifestation of the Divine Being, according to that measure of knowledge which man is fitted to receive, are the themes on which the Bible dilates. Hence there is but little comparatively of theological matter simply didactic in the volume of scripture. The body of divine truth, strictly relating to the Deity, is historical. The mode in which that divine truth is conveyed is for the most part indirect, being imparted incidentally whilst some events—either actually passing, or prefigured in the shadows of prophecy, or sublimed into celestial visions,—are the obvious and immediate business of the narrative. If we consider in what manner we arrive at the scriptural truth of a Trinity in the Unity of the Godhead, it will serve to illustrate these observations. If we except the controverted text of the Heavenly Witnesses *,—if controverted it

* 1 John, v. 7.

may be justly called with so strong an evidence against its authenticity,—we shall find that this doctrine is not dogmatically revealed to us in any express sentence setting it forth to our belief in so many formal terms *; but results rather

---

* The baptismal form has the appearance of being a dogmatical assertion of the doctrine of the Trinity; but is it not so to us, because we connect it with the whole information of scripture; of which, when so understood by us, it forms the only consistent summary?—" Hear, O Israel, the Lord our God is one Lord;" Deuteronomy, vi. 4. is indeed a strong express affirmation of the Unity of the Godhead; but this form of its annunciation may be referred to the peculiarity of Judaism, as a more positive institution of religion than Christianity, and its essential nature as opposed to polytheism and idolatry: or the account of it may be, that this truth does not admit of being clearly revealed in any other form.

The beginning of Saint John's Gospel, and of the Epistle to the Hebrews, and certain passages of the Apocalypse, in which the humble reader of scripture discerns evident intimations of our Saviour's divinity, may perhaps be regarded, (especially the first,) as dogmatical assertions of that doctrine. But this view of these texts would not invalidate the general assertion, that Scripture truths are not dogmatically revealed. For it is evident that these texts imply *certain transactions* on the part of the sacred Person whose nature they unfold, and are meant to guide our conceptions of Him in his *office* of one sent

as a real truth of revelation, from the concurrent evidence of a variety of passages, in which the Deity is represented as performing offices for the good of man under three *distinct* hypostases or persons *. A doctrine established on a footing of this nature, it is important to observe, rests on the most immovable basis. For a single passage, or even several detached passages, expressly asserting any particular doc-

to enlighten and redeem the world. And they cannot therefore be regarded as absolutely *resting* theological truth on mere abstract naked declaration.

* " Ecce dico alium esse Patrem, et alium Filium, non divisione alium, sed *distinctione.*" Tertullian. contra Prax. cited by Hooker: Eccles. Polity, V. 56, Vol. II. p. 227, note, 8vo.

" The profession of a Trinity in Unity is opposed to all who held three Gods, or one God with three names; or who held the Son to be a mere man, or inferior to the Father as to his divinity. The word " *Person* " is not to be understood in its usual sense, but as a term borrowed from common language, and used in a sense not very remote from its usual sense, to express a distinction which must be expressed in some way, and of which we have no clear comprehension." Hey's Lectures in Divinity, Vol. II. p. 243.

See also Justin. Martyr. Quæst. et Resp. ad Orthodox. Qu. XVII. Op. p. 400.

trine, may be interpolated,—may be cavilled at, —may be explained away;—but a truth, to the establishment of which the whole tenour of a volume conspires, cannot be overthrown, without the destruction of the sense of the whole volume itself. Its existence, as a revealed truth, is then inseparable from the existence of the book, which professes to be a record of divine truth. This remark may shew, that it is no imperfection in the scriptures,—as the vain speculatist may suppose, demanding that the doctrines of religion should be established with a degree of evidence which Almighty Wisdom has not judged it necessary to afford,—to convey their divine knowledge in this indirect manner, but rather a valid criterion of the soundness of the instruction so conveyed.

Had the Bible been a treatise on the nature of the Deity, the reverse of that which has been here observed respecting the doctrine of the Trinity, it may justly be supposed, would then have been the case. This divine truth might then naturally have assumed a dogmatic form in the very scriptures themselves, and have been inscribed on the vestibule of their school of sacred lore—instead of being slowly developed, as it is, through a series of progressive dispensations, ultimately converging their light in it as in their focus.

Hence it is, that whilst the mysteries of Christianity contain so much that exceeds and baffles our comprehension, yet they have all a subserviency to that moral instruction with regard to human life, which, we infer, must be a characteristic of the sacred writings—a subserviency, which renders them at once both intelligible* and practical to us. Being constantly enforced as a sublime lesson from some circumstances of human nature, they readily combine with our ordinary conduct, as motives and incentives to duty; and at the same time bestow an elevation

---

* Dr. Hey sometimes speaks of Christian doctrines as "unintelligible", when surely he ought rather to use the word *inconceivable*. If by a doctrine we mean a truth of Christianity expressed in a proposition, it must be so far intelligible to us as the terms employed are understood;—but as it respects things to which those terms are only analogically applied, it must, at the same time, contain inconceivable truth.

on those thoughts of the human heart and those events of life, which they consecrate to the developement of the divine doings.

Let us only remember the animated apostrophe of St. John,—founded on that comprehensive designation of the mystery of redemption; " God is love ":—" Beloved, if God so loved us, we ought also to love one another!" First, we observe, the notion of parental love is transferred from man to the Deity: and then, an inference is drawn from it thus transferred, to the enforcement of mutual benevolence among men. Here then we have a sublime doctrine of scripture, impressed on a sentiment of the human heart; and the practical use which the Apostle makes of it, is,—that we ought, from the very incorporation of this sentiment with the sacred mystery, still more to love one another. That the appeal is irresistible, we cannot but acknowledge. The sentiment of the human heart, thus adopted in the divine communication, reverts with a supernatural force, and a purer flame, to those circumstances of human life from which it was taken.—Or if we look to the precept; "Be ye holy, for I am holy"; here we find a religious truth with its accompanying moral obligation, expressed under ideas which can only belong properly to man; ideas belonging to an act of religion; since holiness implies the setting apart, or devoting, of ourselves,—our persons, our actions, our thoughts,—to the service and glory of God. God is pleased here to inform us, that He is to be regarded as one so set apart, exempt from all common objects of our use or service, and consecrated to religion; and that we must consequently set apart and devote ourselves to God exclusively, in imitation of that transcendental sacredness, which we are taught to ascribe to Him. And how forcibly does this sentiment of man, thus elevated, and canonized amidst the band of the divine perfections, call upon us from its seat in the bosom of God, to come forth from the pollutions of the world,—to make clean the heart,—to present ourselves to God without spot or blemish, as those who have been redeemed, not only from the *punishment* of iniquity, but from *iniquity* itself?

Regarding, then, the scriptures, as engaged in revealing to us the true moral of our present circumstances, and not as an attempt to delineate to us "things which eye hath not seen, nor ear heard, neither hath it entered into the heart of man to conceive"; we must expect to find in them a ready solution of the difficulties of our situation in the world, so far as those difficulties have respect to *conduct*,—a safe and unerring guide to our feet through the mazes of that labyrinth, in which the conflicting passions of our hearts, and the disorders of the world, have involved us. A volume of revelation, thus professedly adapted to our wants and infirmities, directs us to an experimental test of its divine philosophy. Did it fail in this test, we should rightly judge, that it had deserted us in that very point, where we expected that its hand would have stayed us, and its consolations have refreshed the anxious, drooping spirit. We might then justly say of it, as was said of the mere oratorical philosopher: " Artem vitæ professus, delinquit in vita."*

More especially, too, when we recollect, that it is from the inefficient conduct of its professors that our religion receives the greatest wounds to its credit †; that the inefficiency of

* Cicero, Tuscul. Disput. II. 4.

" The book which unfolds it [the Christian Religion] has exaggerated its comprehensiveness, and the first distinguished Christians had a delusive view of it, if it does not actually claim to mingle its principles with the whole system of moral ideas, so as to impart to them a specific character; in the same manner as the element of fire, interfused through the various forms and combinations of other elements, produces throughout them, even when latent, a certain important modification, which they would instantly lose, and therefore lose their perfect condition, by its exclusion.

" And this claim to extensive interference, made, as a matter of authority, for the Christian principles, appears to be supported by their *nature*. For they are not of a nature which necessarily restricts them to a peculiar department, like the principles which constitute some of the sciences," &c. Foster's Essays, p. 382—385.

† " They had also a strong presumptive proof of the truth of it, perhaps of much greater force in way of argument than many think, of which we have very little remaining; I mean,

the nominal Christian is perverted into a charge of inefficiency against the religion itself, it is important to call experience to its aid and confirmation,—to appeal from Christianity *perverted*, to Christianity in its *integrity* and *native beauty* of holiness,—and to shew, that, however the outward aspect of some cases may disparage or contradict its sacred truths; however its confident promises of victory over the world, and of assistance through its various trials, may apparently be thwarted by the malignity of untoward circumstances; it still *is such* as to effect all that it holds out in expectation to the world: —that, as an emanation from the fountain of light, though discharging itself into the tide of human affairs, it yet mingles not with the troubled stream; but flows on, preserving the sanctity of its origin unpolluted in its course*.

The result of these considerations is, that to a

---

the presumptive proof of its truth, from the influence which it had upon the lives of the generality of its professors." Butler's Analogy, Part II. Ch. vi. p. 301.

* Homer, in describing the fabled course of the river Tita-

religion of such a nature as Christianity, the application of the evidence of the natural world is strikingly appropriate and needful. The religion itself calls for the trial,—it challenges the strictest scrutiny into its sublime philosophy; and therefore has a peculiar right to the argument derived from the concurring evidence of experience. If, as will fully appear to all who study "The Analogy" of Bishop Butler, or who prosecute the inquiry by their own observations on the course and constitution of nature, the challenge is satisfied by the result—the coincidence of truth thus disclosed between the systems of nature and grace, can no longer be regarded as something fortuitous; but has evidently been foreseen and contemplated in the very texture of the religion: and therefore must

---

resius, presents us with a beautiful imaginary representation from nature of this moral phenomenon:—

Οἵ τ' ἀμφ' ἱμερτὸν Τιταρήσιον ἔργ' ἐνέμοντο,

Ὅς ῥ' ἐς Πηνειὸν προΐει καλλίρροον ὕδωρ·

Οὐδ' ὅγε Πηνειῷ συμμίσγεται ἀργυροδίνῃ,

Ἀλλά τέ μιν καθύπερθεν ἐπιρρέει, ἠΰτ' ἔλαιον·

Ὅρκου γὰρ δεινοῦ Στυγὸς ὕδατός ἐστιν ἀπορρώξ. Iliad. B. 751.

be received as a coincidence, not simply of *result*, but of antecedent *design*—a design, too, of such a magnitude, and so peculiar in its character, that no other designer but He who ordered the course of nature, He from whom are the outgoings of all things, can have projected it.

Nor is it only, by the force of direct argument, that a philosophical view of Christianity brings conviction to the religious inquirer; but its indirect aid, in clearing away obstructions, and opening a free passage for the entrance of the truth, cannot be too highly estimated. The inquirer is enabled by means of it, to see that many of the things, objected against in Christianity, are paralleled in nature by facts containing like objections; and is thus forced to acknowledge, that, these facts of nature being real, independently of such objections, the truth of the corresponding assertions of the scriptures, is independent of the objections with which they are accompanied. And though the objections against the Christian truths may be stronger in degree than those against the parallel facts of experience; yet, as the real obstacle to the reception of the Christian doctrine is, that there should be *any* objection *whatever* against it; its truth cannot afterwards be impugned on account of the *magnitude* of the objection, when the assumed *ground* for denying the doctrine has been once shown to be untenable*. If, however, the sceptic should perversely maintain that the difference

---

* " Now the observation, that, from the natural constitution and course of things, we must in our temporal concerns, almost continually, and in matters of great consequence, act upon evidence of a like kind and degree to the evidence of religion, is an answer to this argument; because it shows, that it is according to the conduct and character of the Author of nature to appoint we should act upon evidence like to that, which this argument presumes He cannot be supposed to appoint we should act upon: it is an instance, a general one made up of numerous particular ones, of somewhat in His dealing with us, similar to what is said to be incredible. And as the force of this answer lies merely in the parallel, which there is between the evidence for religion and for our temporal conduct; the answer is equally just and conclusive, whether the parallel be made out, by showing the evidence of the former to be higher, or the evidence of the latter to be lower." Butler's Analogy, Part II. Ch. VIII. p. 389.

in degree, whilst the same thing in kind holds both in nature and religion, renders the objection more conclusive against the truth of religion than against the analogous fact of nature; it is easy for the Christian advocate to perceive, that the very nature of analogy requires greater concession to be made to religion, on the score of objection, than to a fact of nature confessedly more limited in its extent.—For example, does the sceptic object to the doctrine of everlasting punishments, as repugnant to his notions of the Divine goodness:—the fact, that punishments by disease, ignominy, and death, are final to individuals in this world, is open, in some degree, to the same objection. Why, may we ask, is not repentance in all such cases available to the suspension of the punishment? Why is it, that there is a time when it is too late; when after the neglect of all admonitions from conscience, from providence, from revelation, the criminal is at length sentenced beyond the possibility of a reprieve?* It must be confessed, that there is a difficulty here in the course of natural provi-

* Butler's Analogy, Part I. Ch. II. p. 56—61.

dence which we cannot entirely remove; it may be infinitely less than the difficulty belonging to the corresponding doctrine of religion, but still it remains a difficulty of the same kind. And while the analogous fact in nature remains *in any degree* unaccountable, the doctrine of religion cannot be rejected, *because* it is unaccountable. But, if it be urged that the difficulty is incalculably increased, when we try to account for *everlasting* punishment; it may be replied, that, by the nature of analogy, everlasting punishment is as credible, under that large system of the divine economy of which the Christian religion treats, as final punishment is in regard to this world; and that the aggravation of the objection, accordingly, is only what might be expected from the peculiar nature of the subject respected in the argument. Or it may be sufficient to state, as a general principle applicable, not only to cases in which greater objections are perceived, but to those too in which we discover no parallel in the course of experience, that subjects of religion must be, by their very nature, *more* liable to objections, than matters of fact*.

This mode of neutralizing the objections brought against Christianity, may little gratify the pride of a speculative curiosity, intruding into mysteries which surpass even angelic intuition; but it is precisely that which will comfort the heart of the humble-minded Christian. He regards objections to his religion as *temptations* to disbelief; and is anxious to find some expedient, by which he may bring the thoughts of his heart into obedience to the doctrine of Christ. To such a person it is all-important to be enabled to see that the objections, with which he may be disquieted, do not tend to *irreligion*,— that they may be allowed to stand in all their force, and yet the religion, which they appeared to threaten, remain true and obligatory on the conduct. It shews that the challenge is absurd and unreasonable, which calls upon the believer in the scriptures to produce an answer to every objection which may be proposed to him.—The

* Page 96.

demand indeed might be argued to be absurd from this principle; that "to answer an objection is a process of discovery"*; and, in religion, of discovery of divine things, which the believer altogether disclaims.—But this argument will not so readily quiet the heartfelt fears of the Christian for the safety of his religion, as to find, that the objections, though unanswerable, are really harmless. Every one perhaps has felt the strong antagonist force of an objection, when he has not had a ready answer to it at his command. However strong our previous conviction may be, it throws a baneful suspicion over all the deductions of our reason. It is so easily grasped too, and recollected in itself, that, with a perverse importunity, it is ever recurring to the mind;—it haunts us at every step; and seems to require exorcism, rather than argument, to lay its mischievous spirit. Here, then, a philosophical view of our religion admirably succours us in this state of

---

* Αἱ μὲν οὖν ἀπορίαι τοιαῦταί τινες συμβαίνουσι· τούτων δὲ τὰ μὲν ἀνελεῖν δεῖ, τὰ δὲ καταλιπεῖν· ἡ γὰρ λύσις τῆς ἀπορίας, εὕρεσίς ἐστι. Arist. Ethic. VII. 2.

perplexity, and restores our confidence in the truth already embraced. It exonerates us from the painful task of racking our ingenuity for a solution of the difficulty in question. Objections, though unanswered, are removed as objections to a supernatural revelation, by appearing also to hold against the creed of the Deist. Let them be insuperable, when separately regarded in their bearing on the facts of the scriptural revelation; by their joint application to both classes of truths,—they are completely neutralized. They resemble the testimony of notorious calumniators, which cannot be admitted to the disparagement of a character reputed for sanctity and worth. So important is the discernment of the coincidence of the systems of grace and nature, if it were only to expose the fallacy of all speculative objections against the truth of revealed doctrines,—thus, to hold up a shield from which the fiery darts of the enemy may recoil with idle impetuosity. As the kingdom divided against itself cannot stand; so it shews that, if reason employs such weapons against revelation, reason is divided against herself, and cannot stand; that, while she is sending her forces abroad for the reduction of a distant territory, she is exposing her own frontier to similar incursions, and the heart of her empire to faction and civil disturbance;—that the same arms, which lay waste the scene of her invasion, will be found effectual to spread the contagion of spoil and desolation at home.

The force with which this evidence of Christianity acts in dissipating speculative objections, has induced some writers to depreciate its general importance as an evidence of the religion; and to consider it more as an engine of defence to the scripture revelation, than as a positive auxiliary in the sacred cause*. But though it

---

* Mr. Dugald Stewart, in his "Elements of the Philosophy of the Human Mind" (Vol. II. p. 423, note, 8vo.), refers to the opinions of Dr. Reid, and Dr. Campbell, on the subject of analogical reasoning, and expresses his "doubts, whether both of these ingenious writers have not somewhat underrated the importance of analogy as a medium of proof, and as a source of new information." "I acknowledge at the same time," he proceeds to remark, "that between the positive and the ne-

is impregnable only in this point of view; let us not therefore slight its aid as a direct persuasive to the reception of Christianity. If it were only for its use in correcting our hasty anticipations concerning the truths of religion, by simply leading us into the right track of inquiry, it would deserve to be enrolled among the strongest confirmations of the direct proofs. But it has been already shewn that it does much more than this—inasmuch as it is, in each single instance,—in which an analogy is discernible between a doctrine of scripture and a fact of nature,—a direct presumptive evidence of the scriptural truth; and, in its cumulative application, is a very powerful argument to the divine

gative applications of this species of evidence, there is an essential difference. When employed to refute an objection, it may often furnish an argument irresistibly and unanswerably convincing. When employed as a medium of proof, it can never authorize more than a probable conjecture, inviting and encouraging further examination. In some instances, however, the probability resulting from a concurrence of different analogies may rise so high, as to produce an effect on the belief scarcely distinguishable from moral certainty."

origin of the whole revelation: and it will further appear, under the next head of our inquiry, to be precisely that kind of evidence, which ought to have an immediate influence with creatures, sent into the world, to act, rather than to know and to debate.

II. We are come, in the next place, to the consideration of the practical importance of discerning a coincidence between scriptural truth and the natural world.—Hitherto we have only estimated the force of such coincidence, as part of the general argument on which an *opinion* of the truth of the Christian revelation is founded. If this, however, were the whole amount of that force, it would not have that commanding efficacy in bringing men to a sincere conviction of the scripture truth, to which a reference has been made in the concluding observations on the last head; and which a further examination of its nature will fully disclose. It might be evaded, as all arguments for religion may be which are merely speculative, with the plea of Agrippa, in his answer to Paul; "almost thou persuadest me to be a Christian." Its claims may be deemed worthy of attention, while that attention is postponed and altogether neglected. In all practical matters, indeed, a speculative view of the subject is in itself insufficient and nugatory. Men will not be satisfied to perceive on which side of the question the truth lies, but they must also be induced to adopt it in action by its connexion with the practical principles of their nature.—Religion, especially, as the grand moving power of human life,—though it must be adopted in sincerity of faith, and on the purest motive of giving glory to God,—looks with such an anxious eye to the conduct of men, that it willingly enlists into its service any argument, which tends, however imperfectly, to make converts to its saving doctrine. It says, in the accents of its Divine Founder; "whoever is not against us is for us";—and it rejoices over even such disciples, of whom it can pronounce no more, than that they are "not far from the kingdom of heaven";—indulging the charitable and reasonable hope, that those who have in any degree experienced the delights of its converse,—who have been only within its outer courts,—will not, without some reluctance, fall back from their course; but will be induced to proceed onward, and eventually to become its disciples indeed.—Hence it by no means disclaims the employment of arguments, grounded on its expediency, and accommodation to the principle of rational self-love. And consequently it demands to be set forth, not only as *true*, but as *practicable*—not only as what we have the strongest reason to *assent to* and *believe*, but what we have also the strongest reason to *act upon* and *obey*.

1. To accomplish, then, this practical aim of religion, a proof of its truth, derived from matter of fact, is of much greater force than the most elaborate and accumulated speculative arguments. However deficient such a proof may be, in not giving a full verification of the parallel doctrines of religion, when those doctrines are regarded only as so many speculative tenets of Christianity—it is decisive as to the adoption of that line of conduct, which the doctrines pre-

scribe, considered as practical principles. For the correspondences of experience exhibit the *principles* themselves of the doctrines in actual operation: and, *practically* to embrace the doctrines revealed, therefore, we have only to believe and to act, as we have believed and acted on former occasions in worldly matters.—For example, the sacred truth of Christ's mediation, if it be regarded simply as a speculative tenet of Christianity, is only partially verified by experience. We find that, in general, we obtain the advantages of life, and relief from its evils, through the cooperation of others—and we can, upon the evidence of this observed fact, readily credit the corresponding grand and consolatory truth of revelation, in that divine acceptation in which it is the object of our faith; though it so far transcends its counterpart in the constitution of nature. But if we look to the practical efficacy of the doctrine—the act of reliance on our all-powerful Mediator—then is the observation of experience, that we are continually placing reliance on the exertions of others in our behalf, unanswerably decisive of the expediency of adopting the doctrine as a rule of life. So again, with respect to the doctrine of a future life:—Compare it with experience, and a *speculative* doubt may remain whether it be true—but, practically, there can be none : as rational beings we cannot but act as if it were true:—because all those instances by which it is confirmed, are instances of our practically *depending* on such a continuance of being as a future life is supposed to be.

Whatever then may be the speculative difficulties attached to any particular truth of Christianity, these difficulties vanish, when the truths themselves are brought home to our bosom, and the question is put to the conscience, " What shall I *do* to be saved ?" They cannot for a moment be suffered to interfere, and to check the course of our action, when this course of action, consequent on the reception of the doctrines, is no other than that on which we have already proceeded. An elevation of thought, and a refinement of motive, may be imparted to our actions ;—they may be performed on a far more magnificent scale, and with far nobler views;—but consistency of conduct requires them to be done *religiously*, as well as *naturally*—with a view to everlasting happiness, as well as to temporal advantage; and their *actual duty* remains unaltered. Their nature may be changed, by the different nature of the end to which they are directed, when they are done from motives of religion; but their *expediency* remains the same.

2. As the expediency of acting upon the instructions of religion, is enforced by a discernment of their conformity with experience,—so also the *practicability* of those instructions is strikingly demonstrated by this test of their truth. —To detract from the novel and unusual aspect of an action is no inconsiderable inducement to its performance. There are cases indeed where the novelty itself of a pursuit strongly stimulates to action: but these are cases, where the work may be adequately performed by sudden and desultory effort—where the force of impact is required, rather than that of regular and continued pressure. Widely different from these is the case

of our religious duties. These are persevering exertions; to which it belongs to be strengthened by exercise, and matured by habit. These require to be so ingrained in the character of the agent, that they may seem to be a part of his very nature, and not to have been forcibly superinduced.—This then is an object towards which this evidence of religion excellently conspires. It removes from the mind the disrelish which might arise against commencing the pursuit of Christianity, as a matter altogether new and unknown to our practice. It shews the religion to be, by no means a setting forth of strange and unheard-of things, but only a continuance of what we have already begun,—an extension of a system of conduct which is already in operation. Thus it imperceptibly allures us to the practical adoption of Christianity even amidst our misgivings and hesitations. We find that, whilst we thought we were pausing on the threshold of the Faith,—weighing the value of objections,—and disputing every inch of our way,—all our scrupulous caution has been superfluous; since we are *in fact* already obedient to the principles which our religion calls upon us to embrace and pursue;—that we have been its disciples in a manner, whilst we were unconscious of it; and whilst we debated it in words, already confessed it in our lives. From such a discovery, the transition is comparatively easy to the hearty reception of the religion in all its spiritual energy. It is not beginning anew. It is but to *repeat*, in order to our *eternal* happiness, what we have been doing through our whole previous life, in order to our *temporal* interests. It is but to carry forward the wisdom of the children of this generation, to the condition of the children of light.

3. The practical cogency of this evidence of a revelation is not, however, to be attributed exclusively to the appeal which it makes to our habitual system of conduct: it is also owing, in a great measure, to the strong personal application of the religious truth which it suggests to us.— The Christian religion, when thus depicted to our view, appears no longer simply, as the religion of the universe at large,—as the senti-

ments towards the Deity, which belong indiscriminately to all intelligent creatures of every order throughout the boundless creation,—but as that part of the general tribute of praise and glory due to the common Father, which is peculiarly appropriate to, and incumbent on man. A distinct and definite character is given to that, which otherwise, in its infinitude, would surpass our reach; or, in its indiscriminateness, might afford a plea of evasion to the generality of mankind, who are little disposed to do what is not personally and immediately their concern. Christianity, by the organ of our experience, tells us, that we are they by whom its duties are to be performed; that we are the creatures of God to whom its message is sent; that it is *our* light, *our* life. By its adaptation in all its detail to our circumstances, it powerfully persuades us, that it is designed for *our* use and advantage. It awakens, accordingly, under this point of view, that active interest which naturally belongs to any thing which appears strictly and peculiarly our own.—The prevailing power of such an interest is strikingly displayed under the partial system of the Jewish dispensation. The great argument for gratitude and devotion to God, which Judaism addressed to its votaries, was, that God had a favour to them above all other nations of the world; that he was the God of *their Fathers*, the God of Abraham, of Isaac, and of Jacob; the Lord who brought *them* forth out of the land of Egypt, and out of the house of bondage: and the sanctions with which it enforced its precepts were, national and personal prosperity on the one hand, national and personal affliction on the other*. The religion was thus made to the Children of Israel eminently their own: precepts were enjoined imperative on themselves alone: and they were stimulated to their performance, not by those transcendant and general views of heaven and eternity, which they would have participated in common with the rest of mankind, but by promises peculiar to themselves, as a chosen race and a peculiar people. And may we not reasonably conceive, that this appropriation of their religion is one among the causes of the inflexible adherence of the

* Page 118.

Jewish nation, both in ancient and modern times, to their prescribed institutions? the personality, if it may be so expressed, of their system of faith, rendering them loth to exchange it for another confessedly more comprehensive and irrespective; which, however attractive in its noble universality, yet to one nurtured in Judaism seems probably, in contrast with his religion, a vague, and cold, and uninteresting creed*.—But to those who can dispassionately consider it, the interest of Christianity is similar in kind, though it embraces a much larger sphere, as the religion of mankind. When contemplated in its connexion with the state of things in which we have our being, it appears invested with a peculiar commission from on high, to call us to a consideration of the ways in which we are walking. It then, to adopt the language of the Prophet, draws us, "with cords of a man, with bands of love"†. And in thus surveying it, we are tempt-

---

* The spread of Calvinism has probably been aided by a similar feeling; as well as that of the belief that there is no salvation for any out of the pale of a particular communion.

† Hos. xi. 4.

ed to exclaim; "Lord, what is man that thou art mindful of him, or the son of man, that thou so regardest him!" or to say with the child Samuel; "Speak, Lord, for thy servant heareth."

4. There is still another circumstance belonging to this evidence of Christianity, which renders it powerful as a practical evidence of the truth revealed. We bear it about with us, as derived from the principles of our own nature; so that it is ever at hand to reinforce our belief, and succour us against the assaults of doubt and incredulity. It requires no labour of recurrence to learned authorities, or of recollection of various arguments, for the establishment of our conclusion. It requires only that we should pause to ask ourselves, how we should think, and how we should act, if an ordinary occasion of human life were the matter in deliberation; and what natural prudence would suggest, is an unanswerable evidence for the prudence of our decision in the question of religion. Thus, to recur to an instance already frequently referred to;—if we are inclined to hesitate respecting the truth of

the revealed doctrine of a future state; we have only to reflect with ourselves,—that our opinion in things of the world is, that they will continue to exist through successive alterations, where there is no adequate impediment to such continuance, and that we constantly act upon this opinion. How can we evade then the argument thence arising, that it is prudent to think and act in the same way in regard to this fact of religion? This is a kind of evidence which is precisely adapted to the rapid flux of human life. We must continually be acting on one presumption, or the other, respecting religion; either upon the presumption of its truth or of its falsehood; and little time is allowed us for the process of antecedent deliberation. A religion, accordingly, upon which it is expedient to act, *is true* to every practical purpose; human life not admitting of those checks and balancings of judgment which are within the province of abstract contemplation. A religion, on the contrary, upon which it is inexpedient to act, *is false* to every practical purpose; for, either the religion, or the constitution of things to which it is applied, must be absurd; the evident incongruity shewing that there is a faultiness in one or the other*: and our inference, of course, must be, that it is the proposed religion which is wrong. So that the evidence to the prudence of acting upon any given religion, is a sufficient test of its speculative truth to beings, situated as we are, whose life consists not in contemplations but in actions; a test which every one bears about with him, as a present help against the perplexities of doubt—an antidote, existing in the mind itself, to neutralize the poison of speculative infidelity.

In point of fact, it is the argument on which the belief of the generality of mankind is exclusively founded, and to which the conviction of the learned ultimately appeals.—For "to the poor the Gospel has been preached", no less in its evidence, than in its consolatory truths. There is no man who cannot appreciate the value of that which consults his wants—his feelings—his desires—his hopes—his fears. And they, who

---

* Τὸ δ' ἀληθὲς ἐν τοῖς πρακτοῖς ἐκ τῶν ἔργων καὶ τοῦ βίου κρίνεται· ἐν τούτοις γὰρ τὸ κύριον. Aristot. Eth. x. 8.

will but give a calm hearing to the religion of Christ within their hearts, find that it does so,—that it is precisely that which their nature requires,—and that, in accepting its instructions, they are accepting truths, to which their hearts respond yea and amen. They do not, perhaps, state thus much to themselves in words; they are not perhaps aware that such a decision in favour of the truth of their religion has been pronounced by their judgment; but the judgment is nevertheless implied in this silent process of inquiry, and the acceptance of the religion so examined is no less sincere and valid, than where it is formally declared by the conclusions of the methodical and learned inquirer.—As to the learned, though these may explore the regions of history, and bring forth the latent evidences of a revelation from every track of inquiry; yet, after all their labours, they must confess, that, without some evidence more immediately touching themselves, and saying as it were to them personally, "O fools, and slow of heart to believe!" the mere historical assent extorted from them would be but a cold and inoperative belief.

The formal examination into the question of the truth of Christianity, tends only to a general decision respecting its merits. The student rises from the discussion, convinced that the religion is worthy of all acceptance; but if he confines his inquiry to such a process alone, his heart remains unmoved, and he straightway forgets what manner of religion that is, whose authenticity he has explored*. For, splendid as the apparatus of miracles and prophecies may be, by which its divine origin is established; numberless as the arguments may be, from considerations of the nature of human testimony, and from collateral proofs; there is nothing in all such evidences which *wins* the *individual* attention of the inquirer. It is charity towards man which must appear, as a characteristic of a divine revelation, to render the religion proposed in it a personal ap-

---

* Ἀλλ' οἱ πολλοὶ ταῦτα μὲν οὐ πράττουσιν, ἐπὶ δὲ τὸν λόγον καταφεύγοντες οἴονται φιλοσοφεῖν, καὶ οὕτως ἔσεσθαι σπουδαῖοι· ὅμοιόν τι ποιοῦντες τοῖς κάμνουσιν, οἳ τῶν ἰατρῶν ἀκούουσι μὲν ἐπιμελῶς, ποιοῦσι δ' οὐθὲν τῶν προσταττομένων· Ὥσπερ οὖν οὐδ' ἐκεῖνοι εὖ ἕξουσι τὸ σῶμα, οὕτω θεραπευόμενοι· οὐδ' οὗτοι τὴν ψυχὴν, οὕτω φιλοσοφοῦντες. Aristot. Eth. ii. 4.

peal to each man individually. And, if it may be allowed so to apply the words of St. Paul, it may be said, that, though it spoke with the tongues of men and angels, though it had the gift of prophecy, and understood all mysteries and all knowledge,—yet if it had not *charity*, it would be nothing. We must feel ourselves to be the objects of the religion's care; as the persons for whom it especially provides. And the learned, no less than the simple and unlearned, must discern this provision in their religion. Whilst it is necessary, for the general defence of it, that they should thoroughly know the strength of the position which it occupies in the historical world,—that they should have gone round the towers, and have marked well the bulwarks of their Sion,—it is necessary for their own instruction, and comfort, and discipline in righteousness, that they should be inwardly sensible of those numberless ties, by which their creed, if freely admitted into the heart, entwines itself with their affections.

III. Thus far the importance of the coincidence between the doctrines of scripture, and facts of nature, has been considered under those points of view in which it appears strictly *as an evidence* to the truth of the scriptures.—Another light, in which its importance will further appear, is, its illustrative application.

It is obvious to remark, that a supernatural revelation must, above all things, stand in need of illustration,—as being conversant about matters confessedly above the reach of human investigation,—and as being altogether different, in the mode of imparting its truths, from our ordinary means of knowledge. Many things must naturally appear in it hard to be understood; many things irreconcilable with themselves and with our previous ideas. For the absence of mystery is one of the strongest proofs of the mere human origin of any presumed revelation. That such a result should be produced, shews, that human art has been employed in smoothing down inequalities, and obviating future objections; whereas, in a true revelation, there will be a bold irregularity, corresponding to that which characterizes the face of the natural world—a sort of careless contempt of the little prejudices and short-sighted cavils of those to whom it is presented. Those only who survey it not with a religious eye,—which in matters of revelation is the eye of true taste,—will wish to see its valleys exalted, and its mountains brought low, and the crooked made straight, and the rough places plain; and the whole reduced to one unvaried mass of level uniformity; not perceiving that it is this very picturesqueness of form which speaks the operations of the great Artificer of nature. It is, as in judging of the works of art. Those who are uninformed in the principles of painting, or deficient in taste, will admire those parts of a picture, in which they perceive an exact resemblance to some well-known object; and either overlook, or even blame, those parts in which the mere work of imitation is less conspicuous. And yet it is in such parts often that the genius of the painter has exerted its fullest power; and distinguished the picture, as the offspring of a mind, transcending the barriers which mere art interposes, and stamping an image of itself on the material employed.

But while mysteries must exist in a divine revelation, and be attended with difficulties which the most gigantic powers of human intellect can never master—still, much may be accomplished towards the alleviation of these difficulties by a process of illustration, which, without attempting to explain the mysterious, shall open the mind to a reception of it.

Nor is it only on account of the real mystery contained in the matter of revelation, that recourse must be had to illustrative reasoning:—but there is moreover a false mysteriousness which accompanies the objects of faith as they appear to the naked eye of reason—an unreal cloud, which conceals from our view their true form, and invests them with the air of phantoms of darkness. We come to the consideration of the divine truths unfolded in scripture, in a state of excitement, and with a sensitiveness of feeling, which is naturally awakened by subjects of such awful and overpowering interest. Hence it is, that we cannot at first duly apprehend them:—in some cases we are disposed to exaggerate the wonder;—in other cases, to recoil from their real and spiritual acceptation, as conveying a knowledge too wonderful for man. Thus we find, in some persons, the mysterious nature of divine doctrine leads to its enthusiastic perversion—in others, to its virtual rejection from their creed, by the freedom of rational explanation. The same cause acts in contrary ways, according to the peculiar temperament of the mind on which it acts. Where the mind is imbued with a false philosophy, and impressed with a fond conceit of the abilities of human reason,—there it produces a rejection of vital religion, under the various shades of the liberal, the rationalist, the sceptic, and the infidel. Where the mind is uncultivated, or naturally ardent and susceptible, or unaccustomed to a severity of control in its imaginative powers,—there we observe its effect in the enthusiast—the mystic—the fanatic—and the superstitious. The former class, when any mystery of revelation is proposed to their acceptance, are ready to ask with Nicodemus—" How can these things be?"—The mystery appears to their eye greater than it really is; because they reflect back on it all their own misconception and ignorance, and thus behold its outline at once magnified, misshapen, and obscured, by the shadows which they have cast around it. So it was, that the doctrine of Christ crucified appeared to the heathen philosopher, foolishness, —and so it is, in these days, that the same doctrine is so extenuated and explained away by some professors of Christianity, as to lose all its sublimity and all its consolation. By the latter class the sound of a mysterious doctrine is only heard to awaken the key-note of their minds,—they eagerly surrender themselves to the impulses of awe and admiration, which become to them the standards of spiritual truth, and rest satisfied with no view of sacred mystery, which does not dilate it to the vagueness of their own extravagant conceits. "Credo quia impossibile est," is the characteristic language of such interpreters of scripture. Witness, to this effect, the manner in which Christ's simple appearance in the world was received by the Jews.

" As for this man", said they on one occasion, " we know whence he is, but when Christ cometh, no man knoweth whence he is." Again, they observed concerning him ; " Is not this the carpenter's son ; is not his mother called Mary; and his brethren, James, and Joses, and Simon, and Judas; and his sisters, are they not all with us? Whence then hath this man all these things? And they were offended in him." They would have liked a more mysterious personage : there was indeed enough of mystery to the eye of rational faith, in his wonderful appearance in the world—though he " came not with observation";—but they were offended, because the mystery did not correspond with their enthusiastic expectations. Witness the same fact, in the many perversions of the Christian faith which ecclesiastical history exhibits ;—perversions, in some instances, resolving the plainest intimations of scripture into mysterious meanings; in other instances, overcharging the truth, sufficiently awful in its simple dignity, with a terror which is not of the Lord.

To dissipate, therefore, an undue estimate of sacred truth, whether tending to an excess or defect of faith, and to produce a truly rational, and, at the same time, an animated sense of scriptural doctrine, a reference to experience cannot but be highly subservient. Its tendency must be to disenchant the religious inquirer from that spell, by which the corrupt imaginations of the human heart chain down the intellect, and paralyse its energies. The philosophic disputant it recals to a more accurate examination of the ground, on which he professes to argue against Christianity, and thus combats him with the choice weapons of his own armoury. The forward zeal of the enthusiast and the superstitious it represses, by shewing them, of what manner of spirit the religion which they distort, is—producing undoubted facts as a counterpoise to their unsubstantial opinions, and circumscribing their wild views within some more definite boundaries.

This illustrative application of the evidence derived to revealed religion from the course and constitution of the world, arises, partly from the nature of analogy in general, as a connecting principle between different facts; and partly from its particular application in the subject of religion.

But, before we proceed further in pointing out the illustrative force of this evidence, it may not be unnecessary to premise, that analogy, as a ground of illustration, is not essentially distinct from analogy as a ground of reasoning. For some may be disposed fully to concede the illustrative use of an appeal to the natural world, as a means of conciliating a favourable hearing to religion, but dispute the argumentative validity of such an appeal. It should be observed then, that, unless that which purports to be an illustration of any thing has a real foundation in nature for the comparison instituted, it cannot throw any real light on the subject to which it is applied. If the point of comparison is assumed, the application of the proposed illustration is only hypothetical, and the subject, in its proper nature, is rather obscured, than enlightened, by the false representation of it. Such, indeed, is the actual effect produced by *fanciful* analogies;—they darken the subject itself to which they are applied, whilst they diffuse over it their own specious colouring: and hence the use of such analogies in ennobling and beautifying subjects which require dignity or ornament.—An instance indeed, on which a just analogy is founded, may in itself be fictitious—as in the employment of parables and fables, or in putting a supposed case,—but such instances are just analogies, because they are instances of some real principle obtained by previous induction, or actual observations embodied in some arbitrary form. They are, in fact, *latent inductions*, or philosophical truths divested of their proper evidence.—The real difference then between an argumentative and an illustrative analogy, each being considered simply as such, consists in the form in which they are discerned. If each of several particulars analogically compared is otherwise known, and they are only brought together by analogy, then they are *illustrations* only of each other. But if certain particulars only are known, and these are employed for the *investigation* of another particular, then are the known particulars *arguments* to the unknown one. But the process of detecting the justness of the analogy is the same in each case. If two or more particulars are illustrative of each other, they must be such as might be *argued* by analogy from each other*. The analogies, accordingly, between natural and scriptural truths, are either arguments or illustrations, according to the view we take of scriptural truths. If we consider the scriptural truths as unknown, and consider what they are likely to be, as counterparts in their system to certain facts in the system of nature, every analogy is then an argument;—if we consider the scripture truths as already established in our belief by other arguments, and as real facts no less than those of nature,—then, by detecting just analogies between them, we illustrate, at every step, the less familiar by the more familiar,—the more secret indications of the divine wisdom by its more open and public manifestations.

* See p. 71, note.

1. Now, analogy is in all subjects the life and soul of illustration. It presents to us the same general truth under different points of view. This property of analogy is in itself a fruitful source of instruction. For though the facts themselves which it connects, may be equally knowable in themselves, it does not follow that they are equally so to different minds. The truth, which casts no direct ray to a particular mind, may be powerfully reflected to it from another truth, to which its peculiar habits of thought have suitably disposed it.—The poet or the orator will more readily perceive the propriety and beauty of a particular effect in painting, or sculpture, or music, if the principle of taste involved in that effect, be illustrated to him in some parallel effect in his own art.—To impress us with some idea of the loveliness of wisdom, or of virtue, the ancient philosophers tell us, that " if wisdom and virtue could be seen with the eyes they would excite an ardent love of themselves"*;—thus referring us to our conceptions of material beauty to illustrate a

* Cicero De Fin. II. 16. and De Offic. I. 5.

parallel fact in a moral or an intellectual subject.—Here also may be mentioned the peculiar interest belonging to that kind of biography which exhibits parallel lives;—for, by such comparisons, the points of character, which perhaps in one of the individuals are not sufficiently prominent, in a separate view, are often seen more distinctly, under a different modification, in the other.

2. Often, too, it is not satisfactory to us to see a truth unfolded to our apprehension, in a single instance only; but, from a tacit conviction of the uniformity of truth, we desire to perceive the instruction, conveyed by any particular fact, depicted also in another instance, differing in some respects from that already before us; so that, from the various lights of different facts concentrated on the point in question, we may form a correct judgment, whether the conclusion obtained from the first instance be a real principle of nature. If, for example, any truth of anatomical science collected from observation of our own species, were discerned also in the structure of the lower animals, we should be sure that it was a general principle of the science,

since we found that it held also, where the peculiar circumstances, in which it was first observed, were wanting.

3. Or again, where there are principles, associated with the real cause of any effect in one instance, which may erroneously appear to be part of the cause; the evidence of another instance, in which the same effect is produced, without the concurrence of the principles belonging to the former one, is important to the forming of a right conclusion.—For example,—the presence of thought, and care, and self-love, in the case of our own preservation, may lead us into the gross error of supposing, that the fact of our preservation is attributable to these principles of our nature, and not solely to the unseen hand of Divine Providence. But let us look beyond our own selves,—let us only consider the lilies of the field how they grow; "they toil not, neither do they spin, and yet Solomon, in all his glory, was not arrayed like one of these." Immediately we observe the same result produced, independently of those principles of our nature, which seem to produce it in our

case; but which are thus eminently shewn to be only subordinate and cooperating causes, whilst the real cause must be traced to a particular, superintending, Providence. — Hence, among the different classes of instances to which Bacon directs the attention of the investigator of nature, he enumerates "*instantias conformes*, sive *proportionatas*" (which, he says, he otherwise terms "*parallelas*, sive *similitudines physicas*"); and, having adverted to the practice of former philosophers in noting and explaining the accurate differences among natural productions, as of little real use in constituting the sciences, he requires, that pains should be bestowed rather in inquiring into, and noting, the similitudes and analogies of things : adding, at the same time, the just caution, that the similitudes should not be fortuitous and fanciful, but be "real and substantial, and merged in nature."*

* "Itaque convertenda plane est opera ad inquirendas et notandas rerum similitudines, et analoga, tam in integralibus, quam partibus: illæ enim sunt, quæ naturam uniunt, et constituere scientias incipiunt.

"Verum in his omnino est adhibenda cautio gravis et se-

4. Or, lastly, the variety which is introduced into any subject by analogical argument, is in itself greatly serviceable to the business of instruction, as giving an attractiveness to the subject, and thus alluring the attention of the learner. For example, in the analogy just ad-

vera; ut accipiantur pro *instantiis conformibus* et *proportionatis* illæ, quæ denotant similitudines (ut ab initio diximus) physicas; id est, reales et substantiales, et immersas in natura; non fortuitas et ad speciem; multo minus superstitiosas aut curiosas, quales naturalis magiæ scriptores (homines levissimi, et in rebus tam seriis, quales nunc agimus, vix nominandi) ubique ostentant; magna cum vanitate et desipientia inanes similitudines et sympathias rerum describentes, atque etiam quandoque affingentes." Nov. Org. Lib. II. Aph. 27.

What are real *instantiæ conformes*, he shews in the instances of an optic glass and the eye—the ear, and places returning an echo—the gums of trees, and gems of rocks—the fins of fishes, and the feet of quadrupeds, or feet and wings of birds, &c. A correspondence in the concrete form of the subjects compared is all that is required, according to him, to establish a real physical similitude—that is, an agreement of particular phenomena in some general observation, or general principle discerned in them; agreeably to what has been stated above respecting analogy; and not an agreement in some abstract generic property belonging to the nature of the subjects.

duced, what a pleasing sketch have we from the vegetable world there brought before the mind's eye, and exhibited in friendly contrast with a mysterious moral truth! How different are the analogous instances, and yet how harmonious! The mind, thus led to the acknowledgment of the truth, obtains, in the act of learning, a delightful relaxation from the continued pressure of abstract doctrinal instruction, whilst it glances off to the contemplation of the plant of the field, and yields itself up a willing convert to the truth, over which such loveliness is diffused.

5. Further, whilst analogy appeals so forcibly to the pleasure of association, it also unites in its effect, as a means of instruction, a pleasure akin to that produced by imitation in the fine arts. These accomplish their purpose, by exciting that admiration which arises from perceiving some effect observed in nature attained under an artificial mode of execution*. An analogous fact may, in like manner, be considered

* See Dr. Adam Smith on the Imitative Arts. Works, Vol. V. p. 243.

as an imitation, under a different form, of another fact to which it is analogous. It is a resemblance, as close as the nature of the subjects, to which they respectively belong, will admit. We are pleased, accordingly, with the detection of such a resemblance, formed, as it were, in spite of the real discrepance of the subjects. The unexpected conformity of the different instances excites our admiration, and disposes us to a ready acquiescence in the truth, whose identity stands forth to our view under an actual variety of representation.

6. But perhaps that force of conviction which analogy, when skilfully employed, brings with it, is owing less to any other advantage involved in its use than to this in particular, that it invests the learner with the character of self-instructor. It holds up to him some acknowledged fact, in which, as in a mirror, he may behold the truth in question; and leaves him to deduce it, almost by observation rather than by reasoning, from that which is brought before him. The mind which is thus illumined, instead of being alien-

ated by the dogmatism of its teacher, or repelled by an assumption of superiority on his part, recognizes in its own former conviction the truth which is introduced under a new garb, and accepts it as a just extension of a conclusion in which it has already acquiesced. It seems indeed to be exerting an act of recollection, instead of making fresh acquisitions of knowledge. That pride, which recoils from the humiliating confession of error, and renders the intellect obdurate against the better reason, is then beguiled into compliance with the arguments of an opponent: and the mind, thus relieved of the burthen of resistance to the truth, seems to say in secret to itself, (as Aristotle observes of the effect of metaphor in some instances,) ὡς ἀληθῶς, ἐγὼ δ' ἥμαρτον*, recanting its error whilst it confesses the truth.

Thus it was, that the discourses of Socrates pro-

* Ἔστι δὲ καὶ τὰ ἀστεῖα τὰ πλεῖστα διὰ μεταφορᾶς, καὶ ἐκ τοῦ προσεξαπατᾶν· μᾶλλον γὰρ γίγνεται δῆλον, ὅτι ἔμαθε παρὰ τὸ ἐναντίως ἔχειν, καὶ ἔοικε λέγειν ἡ ψυχὴ, "ὡς ἀληθῶς, ἐγὼ δ' ἥμαρτον." Rhet. III. 11. p. 355.

duced a ready conviction on the mind of his hearers: since it was his practice in any discussion to lead on his inquirers to the point which he wished to establish, by directing their attention to the most acknowledged facts; this being in his judgment the sure method of argument*. This mode indeed of teaching was with him the natural result of that tenet of his philosophy,—that knowledge was nothing but reminiscence—since, according to this opinion, it was only necessary to put leading questions to a learner to awaken the truth, already, as it was supposed, existing in his mind†.—It is remarkable also, that the two great philosophers, to whom science owes its chief advancement, have frequently employed analogy, as a means of illustration, amidst their most serious discussions. Both Aristotle and Bacon are singularly happy in their use of it.—But the writer who deserves

---

* Ὁπότε δὲ αὐτός τι τῷ λόγῳ διεξίοι, διὰ τῶν μάλιστα ὁμολογουμένων ἐπορεύετο, νομίζων ταύτην τὴν ἀσφάλειαν εἶναι λόγου. Xenoph. Mem. Lib. IV. c. vi. p. 228. Schneider.

† See the Phædo.—Platonis Op. Vol. I. p. 165. And the Meno. Vol. IV. p. 352. Bipont. Ed.

particularly to be mentioned here, as one who has employed analogical reasoning with great force in vindicating the truth of Christianity, is Origen. It is indeed an observation made by him, which appears to have suggested to Bishop Butler the line of argument pursued in "The Analogy"—the observation quoted in the introduction to that work—"that he who believes the scripture to have proceeded from Him who is the author of nature, may well expect to find the same sort of difficulties in it, as are found in the constitution of nature."* In several instances Origen has exemplified the application of this general principle. Does he maintain the credibility of the doctrine of Christ crucified for the sins of the world? He speaks of it as a fact, analogous to the known instances of persons devoting themselves to death in behalf of their country, "in order to avert prevailing pestilences, or barren seasons, or tempests of the sea"†; and asks, whether such instances shall have occurred, and the self-devotion of Christ for the destruction

---

* Philocal. p. 23. Ed. Spenc.
† Con. Cels. Lib. i. p. 25. Ed. Spenc.

of the power of the prince of devils, shall be held to have nothing credible in it. Are the desertion and treachery of our Lord's disciples urged as arguments against his divine authority? Origen reminds the infidel, that similar instances of treachery among their followers have occurred to human chiefs, and further shews, how the receding from any teacher, was no proof of the falsehood of his doctrines, by referring to the fact, of Aristotle having left Plato after having been for twenty years a hearer of that philosopher, and of Chrysippus, in like manner, having left Cleanthes *. Again, in refuting the objections brought against Christianity from the existence of heresies among its professors, he points to the existing variations of opinions in philosophy and in medicine, arguing that as neither philosophy, nor medicine, is rejected, as of no use on that account, so neither should Christianity be blamed on account of its heresies †. Many other instances of this mode of arguing might easily be adduced from his writings.

* Con. Cels. Lib. ii. p. 67.
† Con. Cels. Lib. iii. p. 118, 119.

7. Whilst analogy is the happy instrument of conveying light into subjects in general, it is peculiarly so when employed in elucidating the truths of religion. Here the force of contrast with which it acts, is at the *maximum*. We bring together the things of heaven and the things of earth; and bestow on the most remote and inaccessible objects, some portion of that circumstantial particularity which belongs to those present and visible. To behold truths, in themselves so high above our comprehension, in connexion with those which are familiarly inculcated on us by experience, must call forth our strongest admiration, and powerfully interest us in our religion. Divine wisdom then descends from its ethereal seat, as the assessor of the throne of the Eternal*, and communes with us, face to face, and hand to hand. We find that the subjects of which scripture treats are not chimeras; not creations of the fancy, which have no substantial existence; but things which *are*—ἐν οἷς ζῶμεν †—in which we live, and move, and have our being. It

---

* " Give me wisdom that sitteth by Thy throne." Wisd. ix. 4.

† ζητοῦντές τε ἄλλο τι, ὡς εἰπεῖν, ἢ ἐν οἷς ζῶμεν. Thucyd. iii. 38.

no longer appears to us in the light of a scheme, contrived in the bowers of philosophic seclusion, and addressing itself only to the contemplative and empassioned devotee; like the day-dreams of the Koran, emerging from the gloom and solitude of the cave of Hara; but it shines forth conspicuously as an energizing principle; as a knowledge which is power; as a work of the Lord, carried on in the passing scene, with which we cannot help sympathizing, without doing violence to all the principles of our nature.

8. Further, by the discernment of their connexion with the facts of experience, revealed truths are, in a manner, reduced to a scale to which we are accustomed, and on which we can steadily look without confusion of vision. Transcendently awful in their own sublimity, they dazzle the eye which tries to explore them in their proper sphere. But when shadowed out to our view in the course of the natural world, they appear to assume a μέγεθος εὐσύνοπτον,—a magnitude which the mind can comprise within its field of vision, and by means of which it may direct its thoughts,

as from a right principle, to that height of mysterious wisdom, which is set before us in the dispensation of Christianity. Thus, the great mystery of the Gospel,—the salvation wrought for mankind by the blood of a Divine Redeemer,—is described to us as an *atonement* for the sins of the world. Now experience instructs us that, in general, continuance in a course of folly and guilt, beyond a certain point, is irretrievable by the guilty individual himself; but that the intervention, and severe personal sufferings, of others, have often in such cases been the means, by which he has escaped the extreme consequences of his aggravated criminality. Here then we have an opportunity of forming an estimate of the nature of the universal atonement for sin, by that notion of atonement which is suggested to us on the narrow scale of temporal things. And though this parallel truth of nature is infinitely short of the sublimity of the doctrine of Christ crucified, yet how forcibly does this very diminution under which we then contemplate the doctrine, enable us to dwell upon it with accuracy and steadiness of thought! It gives us something in hand, not indeed in which we may rest satisfied as if we had the *whole* of the mystery, but from which our minds may proceed to a more adequate comprehension of it within the limits prescribed to the human understanding.

9. Another cause of the illustrative force of analogy in the subject of religion, is to be found in that feeling of *home*, which the perception of a coincidence between scriptural and natural truths awakens in the human heart. Christianity is thus brought into immediate contact with us; and whilst we learn it in this manner, we seem to be leaning on its bosom, and listening to its converse, as to the well-known accents of a friend. Insignificant as the things of this world appear to our mature reflection, we still grow up from childhood, attached by numberless links to the objects which surround us; and though often our judgment in the severity of its dictates would tear us away from them, we are still found lingering on the threshold of the school which has trained us up, and clinging with devoted fondness to the prejudices which early association

has endeared*. " How shall we sing the Lord's song in a strange land?" was a natural inquiry from the lips of the captive exiles of Israel, when they sat down by the waters of Babylon and wept at the remembrance of Sion. For, so feels human nature generally. The themes of religion, though full of divine consolation, lose their charm to the mind of man, if separated from all those tender associations which bind us to our home in this world. Hence the prevailing anxiety in the breast of the Christian, to know whether he shall revive and perpetuate, in a future state, those endearments of kindred and friendship, which have been the animation and the solace of the days of his pilgrimage on earth:—an anxiety, which sometimes exhibits itself in an impatience of the scriptural grounds of expectation on that point, rendering us too partial

---

* Καὶ εὐχερέστερόν γε ἄνθρωπος τὰς περὶ ἄλλα συνηθείας, κἂν δυσαποσπάστως αὐτῶν ἔχῃ, καταλείψαι ἂν, ἢ τὰς περὶ τὰ δόγματα· πλὴν οὐδ' ἐκεῖνα εὐχερῶς οἱ συνήθεις παρορῶσιν· οὕτως οὐδ' οἰκίας, οὐδὲ πόλεις, ἢ κώμας, οὐδὲ συνήθεις ἀνθρώπους, εὐχερῶς βούλονται καταλιπεῖν οἱ προληφθέντες αὐτοῖς. Origenes contra Celsum, i. p. 40. Ed. Spenceri.

interpreters of every passage of scripture which can be brought, however remotely, to bear on the subject,—or sometimes, in a still more extravagant form, almost tempting the believer to slight the promised happiness of a future state, if unassociated with this charm of the present life. Of the real force indeed of this sentiment in corrupting the purity of our theological opinions,—in which influence, it becomes to the soldier of Christ, as it were, a kind of *maladie du pays*, seducing him from the ranks of orthodox profession,—we have striking examples, in the heretical doctrines of invocation of saints,—veneration of relics,—and prayers for the dead,— doctrines, which, once introduced and hallowed by religion, take the strongest hold on the affections, so that they must first be torn from the heart before they can be renounced by the judgment. Nor is it always a sufficient counteraction to the influence of our prejudices, that we see their tendency to increase in strength, and the mischief which they may hereafter produce by long continuance in the mind. The present harmlessness of an opinion beguiles us into an acquiescence in it, and a disregard of its future consequences;—we foster its infancy with unsuspecting fondness, whilst it imperceptibly reaches a degree of vigour which we can no longer master*.—The sentiment is, at the same time, to a certain extent, just in the eye of Christianity itself. For though it instructs us, that this world is not our real home, but that our citizenship † is in heaven; yet, from the tenour of its precepts, it evidently holds the present life so important with regard to our eternal condition, that

* " Crescit occulto velut arbor ævo." Horat. Od. Lib. i. 12. See a beautiful adumbration of this moral fact in a splendid passage of Æschylus :—Ἔθρεψεν δὲ λέοντα, κ. τ. λ. Agam. 726—745.

† Ἡμῶν γὰρ τὸ πολίτευμα ἐν οὐρανοῖς ὑπάρχει.—Philipp. iii. 20. Μόνον ἀξίως τοῦ εὐαγγελίου τοῦ Χριστοῦ πολιτεύεσθε.—Philipp. i. 27. The full force of these passages of St. Paul is lost in our translation, from their being rendered by the word *conversation*, instead of *citizenship*. The allusion to Christianity as a peculiar civil institution, was familiar to Greeks, as it was also to Jews; since the polities of the Greek legislators, as well as that of Moses, embraced religion. Hence its adoption by the Fathers. The word elsewhere throughout the Epistles rendered *conversation* is ἀναστροφὴ or ἀναστρέφομαι, except in one place (Heb. xiii. 5,) where τρόπος is so translated.

it cannot discard from its use a natural sentiment, which, though too often perversely indulged and abused, in opposition to its precepts, serves to connect the two states of condition.

It is to this feeling then that the analogy between scripture and nature strongly addresses itself. It diffuses over the whole face of Christianity a character of pathos, such as that which radiates from the sacred person of the Redeemer, when we contemplate Him as the Son of God made man. For, had he been manifested to us as God alone, achieving our salvation by the arm of unveiled omnipotence; how inferior, comparatively, would have been the practical interest to us as men, contrasted with that which is called forth, now that we are enabled to regard him as the Word made flesh,—as in all things made like ourselves,—as a brother, by whom we have access to a common Father. Or had he taken on him the nature of angels, he would still have been too far removed from us to admit of our sympathy with his person. Nothing, in short, but the persuasion, that the Lord from heaven is the second Adam, could have so closely interested us in the things which he has said and done in our behalf. And so it is with regard to the whole substance of the religion developed in the scriptures. If it were *simply* divine in its nature, whilst it no less inspired veneration and awe, it would be deficient in that pathetic force, with which it addresses us as a mixed revelation,—as a supernatural system of faith in its origin, and the objects to which it directs our views,—but natural, at the same time, in its form of communication, and its appeal to the intellect and the heart.

We shall not wonder, therefore, that not only profane, but inspired writers also, have had recourse to analogies in enunciating and enforcing the truths which they taught: and that even our Lord himself should have incorporated, so far as we find he has, this method of instruction, with the revelation of the mysterious doctrines involved in his mission to the world. So full indeed is the Bible of important applications of analogy, that we need not look beyond the sacred volume itself in quest of striking examples of the illustration obtained to revealed truth, from its comparison with the experienced course of nature.

10. Nor, moreover, should that important relation which the evidence, derived to Christianity from its analogy to nature, bears to the essential miraculous attestation, upon which the religion must ultimately be received, be omitted in the consideration of its illustrative use. The miraculous attestation, which to the eye-witness of it carries its own conviction, imposes on the hearer, or the reader, when it assumes a traditional form, the necessity of collecting the strongest probabilities from reason, as a counterpoise to its seeming natural incredibility. For, even among common facts, that which when actually seen, or heard, is perfectly credible, is often most incredible when narrated, and can only be established in general belief, by arguments drawn from the known veracity of the narrator, and the concomitant circumstances *. In examining

* Σχεδὸν πᾶσαν ἱστορίαν, κἂν ἀληθὴς ᾖ, βούλεσθαι κατασκευάζειν

into, accordingly, and determining the truth of Christianity as a supernatural revelation, there is this apparent anomaly involved in the process—that we are seeking *probable* evidence for that, which is confessedly *improbable* in its essential nature. We are engaged in exploring some valid reasons, from established principles, for a collection of facts, which must ultimately, however, be recognized as true in all their real improbability: since, but for this improbability, the revelation would cease to be a supernatural revelation. Now, if the scriptural truths, considered as facts miraculously imparted, be shewn to be the same, in any degree, or to any extent, with those which are made known to us in the ordinary way, by ob-

ὡς γεγενημένην, καὶ καταληπτικὴν ποιῆσαι περὶ αὐτῆς φαντασίαν, τῶν σφόδρα ἐστὶ χαλεπωτάτων, καὶ ἐνίοις ἀδύνατον. Origenes contra Celsum, i. p. 32.

" There is a presumption of millions to one, against the story of Cæsar, or of any other man. For suppose a number of common facts, so and so circumstanced, of which one had no kind of proof, should happen to come into one's thoughts; every one would, without any possible doubt, conclude them to be false. And the like may be said of a single common fact." Butler's Analogy, Part II. ch. II. p. 231.

servation and experience, their apparent historical falsehood may be considered as effectually dispelled.—Indeed, without this pioneering of the way, the truth revealed meets with so great obstruction in many minds, especially in those trained to habits of experimental investigation, that no argument, drawn immediately from our abstract notions of God, or the weight of personal testimony to the occurrence of miracles, is sufficient to overcome that suspicion which attaches to the account of its divine origin. That fundamental principle of our nature—our belief in the continuance of the laws of nature according to their present constitution and order*,—is so essential to all our actions, that it is among the strongest of the principles by which we are actuated. And hence the reluctance, which all feel, to admit the fact of any interruption in the observed course of things. That habitual reliance with which we calculate on the recurrence of known phenomena, would be shaken, and perplexity would be introduced into our whole conduct. If it were possible there-

* Page 5, note.

fore, it would not be expedient, that we should be otherwise than prejudiced against the account of a miracle*. At the same time it is necessary that prejudices of this kind should be obviated in so important a case as that of a message sent expressly from God. And this cannot be done in a manner less injurious to the security of our habitual confidence in the known laws of nature, than by an evidence to the truth of the scriptures, which shews that those laws are rigidly maintained in the substance itself of the revelation; and thus exemplifies some portion, at least, of that which is taught us by miraculous

* " And there would indeed be reason to wish, which, by the way, is very different from a right to claim, that all irregularities were prevented or remedied by present interpositions, if these interpositions would have no other effect than this. But it is plain they would have some visible and immediate bad effects: for instance, they would encourage idleness and negligence; and they would render doubtful the natural rule of life, which is ascertained by this very thing, that the course of the world is carried on by general laws. And further, it is certain they would have distant effects, and very great ones too; by means of the wonderful connexions before mentioned." Butler's Analogy, Part I. Ch. ii. p. 181.

interposition, as capable of being learned by us from the teaching of experience. We then rise from the credibility of the facts abstractedly considered, to a conviction of their truth as miraculously established; without feeling ourselves committed to a belief in miracles unaccompanied by the probability of other circumstances essentially connected with them. Our objection to miracles *in general* may still remain in its full force, while it is removed as to the matter of the revelation in question which the miracles are intended to prove. The scripture truths being acknowledged as internally credible, it then appears irrelevant, to question them on account of the *mode* of their conveyance *because* it is miraculous. The disciple of Christianity, and the advocate of the light of experience, meet, as it were, on the neutral territory of a sound philosophy, and bind in holy league their conflicting evidences:—miracles are shewn to speak the language of truth and soberness; and arguments of reason are converted into tests of miracles.

IV. Are there not however some objections to the application of the analogy of the natural world, as an evidence of the truth revealed; and objections of such importance, as to demand a refutation, in order to the admission of the preceding observations in their proper force?

I. Now, with respect to any objection which may be brought against the evidence as hypothetical and illogical,—this ground of exception has already been considered in a former part of this Essay; where it has been argued, that there must be some common principles, in which the truths of any supernatural revelation, and the facts of the natural world, coincide—which common principles are the basis of the analogy instituted between them. There can be no analogy between subjects which have no one common principle in which they may be said ultimately to agree; because, in such cases, no allowances for actual discrepances of subjects can ever reduce the propositions, belonging to them respectively, under any general conclusion. However we may abstract from their peculiarities, there is no approximation to the same theory, and no reason to suppose, therefore, that there is any analogy between them:—since analogy consists in the transference of some conclusion into other circumstances from those under which it was formed, with the requisite allowance for the difference of circumstances. For example; there is no analogy between the science of mechanics and the philosophy of the mind, or between medicine and moral philosophy, or between mathematics and physiology, —because we have no ground for supposing that the two sciences, in either case, have any common principle whatever in which they agree. But the case is different with respect to the truths of a scriptural revelation and the facts of the natural world. Here the same laws of divine administration are involved in both systems of instruction, and the two classes of truths are analogous to each other, because they evidence these laws only as variously, as may be the effect of the peculiar circumstances under which they are contemplated in each case.

II. Another class of objections to the use of this evidence, founded on its supposed insufficiency, has been admirably refuted by Bishop Butler, in one of the concluding chapters of "The Analogy": in which he shews; that it is far from being derogatory from the value of the evidence, that it does not accomplish more than it does, or come with irresistible force of conviction to the mind;—the question in religious evidence being, not whether it be " satisfactory, but whether it be in reason sufficient to prove and discipline that virtue which it presupposes"*:—that, though it does not directly clear up objections against the justice or goodness of God in the Christian scheme, it is a decisive answer to what is really intended by such objections—the endeavour to prove that the things objected against are *incredible*:—that, if it be sufficient to raise a doubting opinion of the truth of Christianity, this is enough to engage a prudent man on the affirmative side, in a cause of such great importance†.

* Part II. Chap. VIII. page 395.

† This is an argument used by Clarke also, in his "Evi-

There are still other objections; proceeding on the assumption, either that this evidence is; 1. an unnecessary addition to the body of proof obtained from the unimpeachable testimony of the inspired writers: or that it detracts, 2. from the necessity; or 3. from the authority, of a written revelation. These grounds of objection will be considered in order.

III. We proceed then in the first place, to the objection which depreciates the evidence as unnecessary.

It is presumed in this objection, that the clear testimony, whether oral or recorded, to the occurrence of miracles at the delivery of religious truth, is sufficient by itself to induce a full belief in the divinity of that truth. Therefore, it is concluded, the argument drawn from the internal character of the religion is superseded— the mind having previously formed its decision

---

dences of Natural and Revealed Religion", Prop. xv. p. 297. He cites Arnobius (adv. Gentes, Lib. 2.) to the same purport.

upon the merits of the oral or written testimony presented to it.

Now undoubtedly the actual occurrence of miracles proves with a conclusive evidence the divinity of the doctrine which they attest; and if we are only fully convinced that miracles have been wrought in confirmation of a doctrine, we are bound to receive such doctrine, without suspicion, as worthy of all acceptation. But then we must not suppose that the decision, formed upon the evidence of miracles, is exclusive of all argument from collateral considerations. On the contrary, it will be found that, in estimating the fact of the miraculous attestation, additional evidence is collected from every point of view which the revelation presents; and that the assent given to that attestation is the ultimate result of inquiries, which have traversed a wide field of investigation *.

---

* On the relation between the miracles and the doctrine attested by them, Clarke well observes :—

" From hence it appears how little reason there is to object, as some have done, that we prove in a circle the doctrine by the miracles, and the miracles by the doctrine. For the

234   *Objection to the Evidence as unnecessary.*

Let us examine the case of an eye-witness of a miracle performed in proof of some doctrine. If it appears that even an eye-witness does not give his assent to the divinity of the doctrine, *exclusively* upon the strength of the appeal made to his senses, but reasons in the very act of his giving that assent, and only gives it ultimately, because every consideration, to which he

miracles, in this way of reasoning, are not at all proved by the doctrine; but only the possibility, and the good tendency, or, at least, the indifferency of the doctrine, are a necessary condition or circumstance, without which the doctrine is not capable of being proved by any miracles. 'Tis indeed the miracles only, that prove the doctrine; and not the doctrine that proves the miracles. But then in order to this end, that the miracles may prove the doctrine, 'tis always necessarily to be first supposed, that the doctrine be such as is in its nature capable of being proved by miracles. The doctrine must be in itself possible, and capable to be proved, and then miracles will prove it to be actually and certainly true. The doctrine is not first known or supposed to be true, and then the miracles proved by it; but the doctrine must be first known to be such as is possible to be true, and then miracles will prove that it actually is so," &c. to the end of the Section. Clarke's "Evidences of Natural and Revealed Religion", Prop. XIV. p. 230, 8vo.

may resort, conspires with it,—it must be readily conceded that they, who receive the doctrine by tradition, in forming a rational judgment of it, look beyond the actual testimony to the occurrence of the miracles, and take a survey of the whole state of the case, before they assign to the miraculous history its relative importance, as the criterion of the divinity of the doctrine.

The difference between the assent given to revealed truth by the eye-witness of the attesting miracles, and that given to the same truth in its traditional form,—is more apparent than real. We are apt to suppose, that it is enough, to be simply a spectator of some sign from heaven, and that the admiration which the event produces, immediately and irresistibly commands our assent. And so we might suppose, from the readiness with which we judge of the relative distance of objects, that this judgment was the simple result of vision alone, instead of its being, as it really is, a compound process—consisting of a comparison between the senses of touch and sight, imperceptibly carried on in the mind of the observer. But, in either case, we should be equally mistaken, if the rapidity, with which the result is attained, were concluded to be a proof of the simplicity of the process.

Now, the same principle, which accounts for the credibility of miracles as proofs of a divine revelation, also renders necessary the concurrence of other evidences of its truth in the act of deciding upon their credibility.—For why is the word of a teacher believed to be of divine authority, because he is enabled to work a miracle? It is, because we have a natural conviction that all the attributes of God are inseparably united,—or rather, are only different ways of conceiving the Supreme Excellence, whom we cannot represent to ourselves in that perfect oneness which belongs to His nature*. This

---

* "In very truth, all the several attributes of the Deity are nothing else but so many partial and inadequate conceptions of one and the same simple perfect Being, taken, as it were, by piecemeal; by reason of the imperfection of our human understandings, which could not fully conceive it all together at once. And therefore are they really all but one thing, though they have the appearance of multiplicity to us.

principle induces us to think, that, wherever the power of the Creator is displayed, His wisdom and His goodness must also be present; and that, therefore, the worker of a miracle must be commissioned by God to instruct us, and that for some good end. From the same principle, any thing in the character of the teacher, or in the object pursued by him, or in the tenour of

As the one simple light of the sun, diversely refracted and reflected from a rorid cloud, hath to us the appearance of the variegated colours of the rainbow." Cudworth's Intellectual System, Book IV. Ch. iv. p. 652, fol.

"The light of the sun is not in the orb itself what we see it in the rainbow. There it is one candid, uniform, perfect blaze of glory; here we separate its perfection in the various attributes of red, yellow, blue, purple, and what else the subtle optician so nicely distinguishes. But still the solar light is not less real in the rainbow, where its rays become thus untwisted, and each differing thread distinctly seen, than while they remain united and incorporated with one another in the sun. Just so it is with the divine nature; it is one simple individual perfection in the Godhead himself. But when refracted and divaricated in passing through the human mind, it becomes power, justice, mercy; which are all separately and adequately represented to the understanding." Bp. Warburton's Sermons, 8vo, Vol. i. p. 38.

the instruction conveyed, which militated with divine wisdom or goodness,—as in the event of the teacher being an immoral person; or of his pursuing some end of private, or party, interest; or a destructive end; or no end of any important benefit to mankind; or of his teaching evil or absurd doctrines,—any thing of this kind, so palpably irreconcilable with our notions of God as an infinitely wise and good Being, would compel us to mistrust the real presence of the divine power, in so defective an instance of divine pretensions. There would be an opposite and conflicting evidence in the case. There is, in fact, no greater reason for believing in the power of God, disjoined from His wisdom and goodness, than in believing in His wisdom and goodness disjoined from his power. And if evidences of His wisdom, or of His goodness, could be as clearly set forth, and as readily estimated, as evidences of Almighty power, they would as naturally, and as fully, prove, in themselves, the reality of inspiration, as external miracles. Prophecy, when verified by the event, is an illustration of this remark; for then we clearly discern a miraculous wisdom accompanying the gift of the revelation. But this evidence is only adapted to an age subsequent to the actual delivery of the revelation; and, in general, it is evident, that neither the divine wisdom, nor divine goodness, can be accurately discerned by the hearer of revealed truth, so as that he may decide *affirmatively* from them, as tests of the inspiration of the teacher.—These evidences are the privileges, rather, of the patient searcher of the scriptures.—In the morning of revelation they are but as the folded buds, waiting the advance of the day to expand in their full-blown beauty.—On this account, we must rather judge of a revelation, at its original delivery, by their *absence*, than attempt to judge by them as *positive* evidences of its divinity. If there be a satisfactory appearance of Almighty power accompanying its delivery, and nothing in itself, or in its circumstances, irreconcilable with the other attributes of God, the mind acquiesces in the demonstration of power as real, and believes the teacher to be the accredited messenger of God. But this process of examination is quickly and imperceptibly performed where a miracle is actually witnessed. The pretender to inspiration is then before us in his own person;—his character, and his words, are presented to our review at the same instant;—and the circumstances, under which the miracle is performed, are open to our inspection. A witness, therefore, must be incompetent, either from gross ignorance, or the bias of passion, who is not able to form a correct judgment on the instant, of the reality of a miracle as an evidence of divine truth. Pretended miracles, exhibited for any other ostensible purpose than the establishment of divine truth, may be rashly and foolishly believed: but the point here insisted on is, that a miracle, done in proof of a divine authority to teach, must be rigidly scrutinized, *as such*, by the mind in the act of believing it; and that a rational belief in it is the *result* of a judgment, formed upon the aggregate of such particulars, as either appear on the face of the transaction, or are necessarily involved in it.

Many of the miracles recorded in the Bible,

certainly appear to have worked a conviction in the witnesses of them, of the divine interposition in the several instances, by their simple exhibition. We read, only, that Jesus " manifested forth his glory, and his disciples believed on him"; or, that when the men " had seen the miracle that Jesus did, they said; this is of a truth that Prophet that should come into the world"; or like expressions, signifying the readiness of the assent which the miracles obtained.—But, from the concise narrative of the scriptures, we could not expect to find a detailed account of the impression produced on the mind of the spectators.—There is, however, one miracle, in which we have more particulars recorded, than are given in general, of the mode in which it operated in producing a belief of the divine authority of the worker of it;—the miracle of the opening of the eyes of the man born blind. Both, the Jews, who were *unwilling* to believe the fact of the miracle having been really performed by Jesus, and the cured blind, who fully believed Jesus to be the worker of it,—employ a *reason*—the former, to account for their disbelief, the latter, to account for the firmness of his belief in it. And the reason is the same in both cases—that God heareth not sinners. The Jews concluded, that Jesus could not have been heard by God in the alleged instance, because, as they said, they *knew* him to be a sinner*;—though, indeed, there was a di-

---

* " Therefore, said some of the Pharisees, this man is not of God, because he keepeth not the sabbath day. Others said, how can a man that is a sinner do such miracles? And there was a division among them." John, ix. 16. Just before this miracle, he had made the assertion, " Before Abraham was, I am"; which the Jews had understood to be an assumption of the prerogative of Jehovah, if not of that sacred incommunicable name itself; since they attempted to stone him for it. On the occasion of another miracle, it is said: " Therefore the Jews sought the more to kill him, because he not only had broken the sabbath, but said also that God was his Father, making himself equal with God." John, v. 18. See also John x. 33. In order indeed to obtain a sentence of death against him, the Jews appear to have appealed to Leviticus xxiv. 16, the law against blasphemy—but may it not be reasonably supposed, that they were *in their hearts* offended at his claim of equality with God, because it appeared to them as an infringement of the Divine *Unity*, and therefore a sin against the *first* commandment of the Decalogue?

vision among them, some arguing, as the subject of the miracle did, that the worker of it could not be a sinner. The man who had been cured, avowed that he knew not, " whether Jesus were a sinner or no"; of this he was assured, that he was *really* cured of a natural infirmity; urging the result, as shewing, that any objection to the reality of the miracle, arising from the sinfulness of the supposed agent, did not apply in that particular case. Evidently, from the tenour of his answer, it may be inferred, that, had he known any thing in the character of Jesus, to set against the *appearance* of supernatural power, he would have felt a perplexity in regard to the reality of the miracle, similar to that which the Jews felt in consequence of their prejudices against Jesus. Because he knew nothing adverse to a favourable construction of the act of Jesus, he regarded it as a real indication of the presence of God with his healer.

The separation, indeed, of the miracles, from the internal evidence of the religion, in favour of which they are alleged, is to impute to them, *per se*, a demonstrative force which they cannot really possess. They are, at most, only *highly probable* evidence of the reality of a divine commission, even to the witness of them. For, first, and directly, they *prove* nothing but power:—it is a subsequent inference,—that the power so exhibited is *divine*,—deduced from the consideration, that no subordinate agent could interfere with the order of the creation—that order which, we must believe, to be not only instituted, but also continually sustained by divine power—without the sanction of the Creator :—and then, it is an inference still more remote, that the words, which the worker of the miracles declares, are the words of God; for we appeal to the principle, that God would not delude his creatures by an invincible temptation*, or *appear* to be with a teacher whom he had not commissioned to teach. So that the certainty of an inspiration, vouched by miraculous evidence, depends, in part, upon the certainty of the intermediate principles, which we assume, in order to bring

* See Cudworth's Intellectual System, Book I. Ch. iv. p. 709, folio.

that evidence home to the case, in question: and, as these principles are only highly probable, it follows, that the conclusion,—that the miracles, supposed real, prove the religion attested by them—is in itself only highly probable: and an evidence of such a nature, admitting of degrees, requires to be substantiated by accompanying evidence, derived from the internal character of the religion, as well as by every collateral proof *.

It ought also to be observed that miracles must not be regarded simply as acts of power, but as implying an ἦθος,—a particular character, in the doer of them. We might see works of power, surpassing the ability of man, performed by inanimate agencies, as in the phenomena of electricity, in which there is evidently nothing beyond the physical result itself †. But it is not so, with

---

* See Archdeacon Powell's discourse on John, v. 36, explanatory of " the Use of Miracles in proving the Divine Mission of our Saviour and his Apostles." Powell's Discourses, p. 102.

† There is no ἦθος in such pretended miracles as the liquefaction of the reputed blood of St. Januarius, annually exhibited

regard to a wonder wrought by the hand of man. Here there is evidently, besides the physical effect, an indication of a *moral* end. Awe and veneration of the Creator and Governor of the world are excited by it.—A miracle is a vehement prayer in act.—We behold a moral creature engaged in a solemn appeal to the God of heaven and earth. The person concerned in it appears invested with a character of extraordinary piety. And we cannot look with indifference on so awful an intercession with the Deity.

at Naples. A chemical process alone is evidenced, and it is no more adapted therefore to produce the proper effect of a miracle on the mind, than any common experiment in natural philosophy.

Origen, in refuting the cavils of Celsus, refers expressly to a connection between moral improvement and the gospel miracles: he admits that, without this accompaniment, the miracles in themselves might not be distinguished from works of magic:—τοῖς ἀπὸ μαγείας ὅμοιοι τὰ περὶ Ἰησοῦ ἱστορούμενα· καὶ ἦν ἂν ὅμοια, εἰ μέχρι ἀποδείξεως ὁμοίως τοῖς μαγγανεύουσιν ἔφθανε δείξας· νυνὶ δὲ, κ. τ. λ. Con. Cels. I. p. 53. The words of Moses, Deuteronomy xiii. 1—5, "If there arise among you a prophet", &c. refer the Israelites to a like criterion of the force of miracles. And so in other places of scripture, we find immorality of teaching connected with *lying wonders*.

It is therefore necessary that every circumstance in his words and actions, should harmonize with the impulse of devout admiration already given to our affections.—Of the influence which such conspiring particulars must have had in an estimate of the credibility of our Lord's miracles, we, who only read the accounts of them, can have no adequate conception. There are many such particulars indeed incapable of being handed down in any record. We should have *seen* him going about doing good, and marked the expression of his countenance, his gesture, and his tone of voice. Had we beheld his tears over the dead Lazarus, or heard the sigh breathed from his soul when he opened the ears and loosed the tongue of the deaf and dumb; we might have contemplated the miracles done on those occasions, with an ardency of feeling which is now utterly inconceivable to us. Those holy individuals with whom he familiarly conversed, enjoyed singular opportunities of appreciating the sublimity of that amiableness which resided in him, and must accordingly have been the most fitly disposed for a right estimate of his miracles.—But we are not left to learn the moral character of his miracles merely by inference. That they were acts of devotion, he has given express intimation by the prayer to the Father, which introduced the raising of Lazarus; and by that remarkable declaration to the disciples concerning the cure of the demoniac child;—" this kind goeth not out but by prayer and fasting."

If, accordingly, it must be conceded, that an assent to revealed truth, founded on the testimony of a miracle done before the eyes, involves an attention to the other circumstances of the revelation; such an examination becomes still more necessary when the revelation assumes a traditional or scriptural form. The way in which it then presents itself to us, is not simply as the word of God, to be believed on the sanction of His power, but, collectively, as an account of a special manifestation of all the divine attributes. We are required, therefore, to decide, upon a separate examination of each attribute as there developed, whether the volume, containing such an account, ought to be received by us as the gift of God. If, had we seen the miracles attesting the Almighty Giver of the truth, we must yet have glanced off from the evidence thus outwardly displayed, in order to guard against a rash ascription of the event to the interposition of God—still more, when the miracles are not seen, but become matter of record, must we beware, that we do not believe them to have really occurred, without concurring evidence of those other divine attributes, which must have been associated with the display of miraculous power, if that power were real.—And the argument accordingly derived from the analogy of nature becomes indispensably necessary. It is an ingredient in our belief of the miracles themselves.

IV. But whilst this evidence may be allowed to be necessary, as a means of preparing the way for the due reception of the miraculous testimony, yet it may be thought, that to accustom the mind to dwell on it, as a valid criterion, in itself, of a revelation from God, has a tendency, either to weaken the conviction of the necessity of a supernatural revelation, and thus to undermine one of the strong grounds of argument against the infidel,—or to detract from the commanding authority of the written word, and introduce a covert infidelity into the very sanctuary of the faith.

How little the necessity of an extraordinary revelation of the divine will is superseded by this evidence, will appear, from reflecting on the *nature* of it. As being only a presumptive evidence of the doctrines revealed in the scriptures, it points to the absolute need of some divinely-commissioned Teacher, to remove the vail upon the heart, and to substantiate and perfect the system of natural theology. In reasoning by analogy to the doctrines which may probably be found in any authentic supernatural revelation, we confess, at the outset of our inquiry, that the regions of Divine Providence into which we attempt to penetrate, lie deeply embosomed in shadows impervious to human sight, and that our clearest anticipations therefore of the things belonging to them, must be pronounced with trembling caution, and, it may be said indeed, with a pious distrust. The Christian Philosopher accordingly does not attempt to philosophize *independently* of the Bible. He does not venture to commit the frail bark of his reason to a sea, wherein no mortal navigator has ever made soundings, and to winds, to which " canvass woven in earthly looms" has never been spread, without taking with him the chart and compass of the Divine Word, and steering by the faithful observations there recorded. The book of nature he takes only as his "*Principia*" of divine philosophy; and endeavours to carry on the elementary knowledge thence obtained, to the illustration of the more recondite truths of Christianity. "Verily, thou art a God that hidest thyself", is a good confession of his Faith, which he never practically forgets.

But does not a view of our religion, identifying to some extent its truths with those of natural theology, lower, in a great measure, the value of its supernatural instructions, by suggesting the idea, that, if so much of revealed knowledge may be learned from the teaching of nature, we have sufficient light to guide us through life in experience alone?

It is certainly a difficult task to divest ourselves of any particular portion of the knowledge present to our minds, and to return to that state in which we were previously to all external and derived information. This difficulty is perceivable in regard to the component parts of our natural stock of knowledge. We are not always able to distinguish between truths, which we have acquired by our own observation, and those communicated to us by others, or learned from books. So it has happened in the comparison of natural and scriptural theology. To all who have been educated under the light of an express revelation (and if the scriptures be true, there has been in fact a supernatural revelation from the earliest period of the world, so that no portion of mankind, no age, however dark, has altogether wanted the benefit of a direct instruction from God), the highest truths of their religion are made as familiar as the most elementary, and are received into the mind upon the same footing of authority. With each truth imparted out of the mass of knowledge promiscuously floated down the stream of human tradition, there is no accompanying specification of the source from which it was originally obtained:—and it is the labour, accordingly, of subsequent investigation to discriminate, by reference to the principles of our constitution, between the possible discoveries of reason, and the wisdom which has expressly descended from above. Thus it is, that opinions have been different respecting the line of demarcation between natural and scriptural theology. Each in its turn has been represented as encroaching on the other. By some, the basis of all evidence to the truth of any scriptural revelation has been destroyed, by their denying to natural theology even the most elementary truths of Divine Science;—whilst, by others, the light of natural theology has been kindled with furtive embers from the altar of the scripture-revelation, and made to glow with a brightness not its own *.

* " For it is not to be imagined that men fail to profit by the light that has been shed upon them, though they have not

But the labour of separating the truth, as it belongs to the scriptures, from that which is properly referable to the stores of nature, must not deter us from the task, or induce us indolently to confound their respective claims. If we closely attend to the principles of our constitution, and thus learn what part of our divine knowledge is properly natural to us, we shall neither think that God has left Himself without witness in the world, nor that He has given us no reason to expect a further revelation of His will. Whilst we believe in Him from the dictates of natural piety, we shall be inclined to pray, that He would help our unbelief, and guide us by His spirit into all truth.

Supposing, for example, that we concede the

always the integrity to own the source from which it comes; or may turn their back upon it, whilst it fills the atmosphere around them; no, not even if in a higher strain of malice, they address the great luminary, only, as the apostate Spirit once did, 'to tell it how they hate its beams.' The fact is not to be denied; the religion of nature *has* had the opportunity of rekindling her faded taper by the gospel light, whether furtively, or unconsciously taken." Davison's Discourses on Prophecy, p. 8.

doctrine of a future life to the discovery of unenlightened reason, we shall be careful so to concede it as not to obliterate its Christian form and expression. If we believe that natural theology bids us hope for a life beyond the present; we must remember, that it is Christianity *alone*, which tells us, that both soul and body will survive the event of our mortal dissolution, and that death shall have no more dominion over us: and thus, we shall maintain the full importance of the scriptural information. For, not to dwell on the comparative certainty of the scriptural message, how great is the difference introduced into the practical view of this doctrine, by the addition of these two important circumstances—the reunion of the soul and body; and the perpetuity of that reunion? If the body shall hereafter be raised again, the body must be kept pure and prepared for its spiritualized condition, as the incorruptible partner of a glorified soul. If there be no change from that state of being which follows the present, —awfully responsible is our present condition, as relative to its unbroken, *eternal*, sequel;—

how much must be done by us *now*, on this side of the grave,—and with what seriousness—what intensity of exertion—when our actions are appointed to live beyond the fleeting moment of their performance ; when their consequences extend through an existence to which we can assign no limits.—So that it is far from being unimportant to us to have our thoughts elevated to a future life, in the full scriptural acceptation of that doctrine. And, however confidently therefore we may rely on the fact of our surviving the shock of death, as a truth of natural theology, we still see the necessity, in order to a prudent conduct of ourselves, that a future life should have been revealed to us *through Him* who is the resurrection and the life ; and who thus appears *alone* to have brought life and immortality—life and immortality in their proper relation to the creature interested in them—to light by his Gospel.

The same argument, indeed, which would lead us to conclude that Christianity is unnecessary,—because we learn many of its truths from nature,—would be equally conclusive against it as the crown and consummation of Judaism. For, as clearly as the prophecies, and types, and precepts of the old covenant, were only shadows of the good things to come under the new covenant—the speculations and conjectures, which reason forms from the facts of experience concerning the things which belong to God's invisible Providence, are only the shadows which foretell the rising of the sun of revelation. And as the Jew, who devoutly bowed his neck to the bondage of the Law, and yet aspired to the better inheritance of another Canaan—even an heavenly one, in which that bondage should be no more,—was disposed, (as we behold the pious Simeon,) to receive the salvation brought by Christ, and no longer to rest satisfied with a system of religion, whose independent obligation had then passed away*: so the truly devout Deist—he who has heartily accepted the information which nature gives him concerning God, and, at the same time, justly learns from her in-

* In reference to this point see the excellent observations of Mr. Davison, on the state of religion, as it was moulded by the Law. Discourses on Prophecy, Disc. IV. p. 157—212.

S

structions to hope for a clearer and more intimate knowledge of the divine doings,—is one who will acknowledge, with humble gratitude, the gift of an authentic supernatural revelation; and will thenceforward no longer regard his experience as a self-sufficient and ultimate organ of divine wisdom. Christianity certainly will not appear necessary to those who are insensible to their real want of it:—so neither did the Jew, who blindly reposed in the privileges of Judaism, and prided himself in his legal purity, feel the necessity of embracing evangelical righteousness; and when Christ therefore came to his own,—to those who were specially invited by a preparatory religion, to expect him amongst them, as "a minister of the circumcision for the truth of God, to confirm the promises made unto the fathers,"—his own received him not—rejected that very person, to whom the whole providential scheme of their religion expressly directed their view.

V. The last objection adverted to remains to be examined; namely, that the evidence here consi dered has a tendency to impugn the paramount authority of the scriptures, as a code of instruction, from which there is no appeal, and whose guidance we must implicitly follow.

It is very possible, that the application of this evidence to the elucidation of scriptural truth may be abused. Not to dwell upon the extreme case of those who have interpreted Christianity by the theories of an hypothetical philosophy*,—

* " Eodem etiam spectant (licet diverso modo) eorum commentationes, qui veritatem Christianæ religionis ex principiis et auctoritatibus philosophorum deducere et confirmare haud veriti sunt; fidei et sensus conjugium tanquam legitimum multa pompa et solennitate celebrantes, et grata rerum varietate animos hominum permulcentes; sed interim divina humanis, impari conditione, permiscentes." Nov. Org. Lib. i. Aph. 89.

With these strictures on the injurious application of philosophy to Christianity, should be joined the following passage of the same author, setting forth the value of a faithful investigation of nature, in order to religious knowledge.—By natural philosophy, it must be remembered, Bacon intends to express the principles of all science, as it is, according to him, " magna scientiarum mater."

" At vere rem reputanti, philosophia naturalis, post verbum

for such interpreters of the scriptures have no concern with the argument drawn from the analogy of nature,—there may be some who carry their philosophizing spirit so far, as to receive nothing, as part of revealed truth, to which they cannot find actual confirmation from some fact of nature. Thus they may proceed, not only to curtail the scriptures of several of the doctrines contained in them, but to limit and diminish those doctrines which they do accept, upon the principle of bringing scriptural truth to a more philosophical standard. Those who thus handle the evidence obtained from the facts of nature, proceed indeed on juster grounds, when compared with the Platonist and the Scholastic theologian; but by their abuse of those grounds, they render their application of the evidence no less hypo-

Dei, certissima superstitionis medicina est; eademque probatissimum fidei alimentum. Itaque merito religioni donatur tanquam fidissima ancilla: cum altera voluntatem Dei, altera potestatem manifestet. Neque enim erravit ille, qui dixit; *erratis, nescientes scripturas, et potestatem Dei:* informationem de voluntate, et meditationem de potestate, nexu individuo commiscens et copulans." Nov. Org. Lib. I. Aph. 89.

thetical than the proceeding of the former. It is mere hypothesis to assume that *all* the truths of a supernatural revelation, must be capable of being inferred by reason from experience,—or to conclude that any particular doctrine cannot be true, because we do not see, independently of scripture, that it *may be* true. To attempt, accordingly, to limit and explain away divine truth by such a mode of reference to the facts of experience, is not to philosophize rightly concerning it. And where we perceive the evidence so unfairly applied, we have only to expose the futility of the pretension to its support, by urging that, whilst we have sufficient data for ascertaining the natural credibility of some doctrines, the same data do not authorize us to decide on the *limits* of credibility.—The facts developed by the scriptures and by experience, being presupposed indeed to be equally taught by God, and therefore of independent authority in themselves—to apply the evidence of experience to the purpose of assimilating the two classes of facts, is contrary to the supposition on which the inquiry proceeds; as it is to assume, that a supernatural revelation has no independent authority.

But from such cases of its abuse, let us turn to consider the effect which the right use of the evidence has on our faith in the written word.—The true Christian Philosopher will take the facts of the scriptures, *as they are written*, without any exception, diminution, or alteration whatever. He will not rashly assume to himself any liberty as a reader of God's word, which the palpable nature of the case precludes his venturing to assume as an observer of God's works. As he cannot accordingly bend and shape the facts of the visible world in conformity with any preconceived theory, or as the capriciousness of fancy may dictate—but must receive, and believe them, and reason from them, as they really are,—he will in like manner consider the truths of the scriptures, as unsusceptible of any modification from his own mind—as facts no less rigid than the phenomena of the natural world;—and receive and believe, and reason from them, as they are written by the finger of God.—Hence, while the argument from the analogy of nature, when rightly employed, represses idle speculation concerning the truths of religion beyond the actual evidence of experience, it does not afford any just pretext to the theologian, for limiting, or varying, any express intimation of holy writ, so as to accommodate it to that morbid fastidiousness of taste, with which some persons regard every thing belonging to supernatural revelation. It does not send him to the natural world to learn a rational interpretation of the scriptures,—or to the scriptures to acquire elementary truths of theology, which philosophy may afterwards carry forward and perfect:—but, on the contrary, to the natural world for the elements of Divine Science,—to the scriptures for its ultimate and sublimest truths;—to the study of the unwritten word of God, that he may have a more lively perception of the written word, as it is written.

The difference between the argument from the analogy of nature, and that which is founded on the reasonableness of revealed truths, has been noticed in an early part of this Essay; but some further observations on this point seem to be required here, in order to acquit the argument from analogy, of that charge of encroachment upon the authority of scripture, which it may incur from being confounded with the latter.

Now the credibility of Christianity as a collection of facts is totally distinct from its reasonableness as a system of religious truths. On the whole indeed, if its particular facts be credible, the general credibility resulting from thence establishes the reasonableness of the religion. It is shewn to be such as reason ought to accept. But when we speak of the reasonableness of our religion, we mean more particularly to assert that it is such as is capable of being established upon the principles of liberty and moral fitness. Whereas its credibility is not at all dependent upon its accordance with these principles, but rests simply on its apparent truth as a matter of fact. It may be credible and yet apparently repugnant to these principles; for the simple observation of similar facts in the course of the world is all that is required, in order to its credibility:—but such an observation tells us nothing respecting the *nature* of the religious facts, and leaves any difficulty belonging to them from abstract considerations of their nature altogether untouched*. It may again be exhibited in accordance with the principles of liberty and moral fitness, and thus be perfectly reasonable and yet appear naturally incredible—for, whilst we abstractedly argue its truth, we only prove that it *ought to be believed;* we produce no outward signs of its truth,—and the non-appearance of any such signs leaves the truth, however cogently inferred, in all its natural incredibility. The difference, in short, between the two lines of argument, lies in this point.—When we argue the credibility of Chris-

---

* It is not only in religion, but in other subjects also, that the reasonableness and credibility of a fact may be opposed to each other:—a strong instance to this effect, is the omission by the ancient Persians of parricide in their list of crimes, on the principle that it was not in the reason of the thing (οὐ γὰρ δή φασι οἰκὸς εἶναι) that a father should die by the hand of his own son, but that, in an apparent case of such a murder, it would be found that the supposed child was not the real offspring of the deceased. Herodotus, Clio, 137.

tianity, we shew its probable truth *without*, or independently of, the reason of it.—When we argue its reasonableness, we infer its probable truth *by* the reason of it.

Both arguments thus terminate in probability; but it is a probability of a different kind which properly belongs to each. Conclusions in favour of the natural credibility of scripture truths are of that kind of probability which is expressed more appropriately by *likelihood*: whereas, those which enforce the reasonableness of scripture truths are probable, according to the proper sense of that term—such as, when contemplated in themselves, are capable of being resolved into principles which the understanding approves, or are deducible from established theories*, or are the *logical* consequences of presupposed facts.

* The difference between the two arguments is that which Aristotle has pointed out, as existing between εἰκὸς and σημεῖον. Arguments drawn from εἰκότα have nothing of the *nature* of *evidence* in them; whereas those which are drawn from σημεῖα appeal to matter of fact, and are evidences more or less conclusive, according to the nature of the facts adduced: (σημεῖον δὲ βούλεται εἶναι πρότασις ἀποδεικτική, ἢ ἀναγκαία, ἢ ἔνδοξος), that

To give examples of this difference of the grounds of probability in regard to the same species of them which he denominates τεκμήριον being unanswerable proof. It is probable that a person has committed murder, whether we argue from his passionate temper, or from his being discovered with blood on his clothes:—but in the first instance we argue from an εἰκὺς; we do not pretend to offer a *proof* of *the charge,* but a reason, or ground of opinion, that *such* a charge may be true;—in the last instance we argue from a σημεῖον; we produce some fact as connected with the event in question, and conclude the event to be established according to the apparent connexion between the fact produced and the event in question.—Thus, Bacon in speaking of the defects of the old philosophy, first adduces the *signs* of its imperfection—such as the people among whom, and the age in which, it originated—the little fruits which it had produced, &c.; and then proceeds to the causes, or reasons, of that imperfection—such as the shortness of the period out of the past ages propitious to the advancement of science—the comparative neglect of natural philosophy, &c.—So, also, a revelation is probable, whether we argue from the insufficiency of natural light—or the goodness of God,—or the morality of it,—or the candour, patient endurance, &c. of its professed messengers—all which circumstances are εἰκότα or grounds of opinion concerning the truth of the revelation:—or, on the other hand, it is probable if we argue from the previous revelation of God in the natural world, as containing σημεῖα of

doctrine of scripture.—A future retribution may be argued; either from those facts of nature, pre-

its truth, or facts which, as far as they go, demonstrate, or rather *indicate*, the truth of it. See Analyt. Prior. II. Ch. XXIX. p. 425, and Rhet. 1. 2.

Mr. Blanco White, in his " Practical and Internal Evidence against Catholicism", has very clearly stated the difference between the two kinds of probable arguments. " Now, the fact is", he observes, " that *probable* and *likely*, though used as synonymous in common language, are perfectly distinct in philosophy. The *probable* is that for the reality of which we can allege some reason; the *likely*, that which bears in its face a semblance or analogy to what is classed in our minds under the predicament of existence." To which the following remarks are subjoined in a note: " Likely is the adjective of the phrase, *like the truth, simile vero*. It is strange that the English language should not possess a substantive answering to *le vraisemblable*. The use of *improbable* to denote what in that language is meant by *invraisemblable* is incorrect. When the French critics reject some indubitable historical facts from the stage, because they want *vraisemblance* (likelihood), they do not mean to say that they are *improbable*, or deficient in proof of their reality; but that the imagination finds them *unlike* to what in the common opinion is held to be the usual course of events."

Historical facts, however, it should be remarked, as such, are neither *probable* nor *likely*. They are simply either true

viously adduced in examining into the justness of the analogy stated between this doctrine and

or false; as matters of experience are simply real or unreal. Aristotle, accordingly, does not limit the imitation of the poet to the description of those actions only which have likelihood in them, but only requires, generally, that the actions represented should be probable. It is the part of the *philosophical* historian to exhibit the facts which he relates, in their probable light. But such a speculation does not belong to him properly as an historian, in which capacity he only relates true or false particulars. Διὸ καὶ φιλοσοφώτερον καὶ σπουδαιότερον ποίησις ἱστορίας ἐστίν.

The application moreover of a common term to both kinds of probability is not peculiar to the English language, for we find that even in the Greek the distinction adverted to by Aristotle between εἰκὸς and σημεῖον is not observed in general, but εἰκὸς is employed to designate any probable argument, whether derived from fact or from the reason of the thing;— and sometimes the characteristic expressions of each kind are joined together, as in the phrase "πείθεσθαι τοῖς εἰκοσί τεκμηρίοις." Euseb. Dem. Ev. p. 133. Aristotle himself uses εἰκὸς in this common sense, where he speaks of the events which are the proper subjects of the poet's art, as being οἷα ἂν γένοιτο, κατὰ τὸ εἰκὸς ἢ τὸ ἀναγκαῖον: adding, that even though the poet should introduce real events, he would not be less the poet on that account, since some real events may be such οἷα ἂν εἰκὸς γένεσθαι. Poetic. Buhle, 219.

the facts of nature*; or from reasons, which would satisfactorily account for it,—derived from the nature of virtue, and our notions of the Divine attributes; combined with the fact, that these reasons do not take effect in the *present* life.—By the first mode of argument we pass on immediately from an evident sign, to that of which it appears to be a sign—from what appears, either the commencement, or part, of an event, or in some way connected with an event, to the same event in its complete and perfect form. We do not resort to any recondite considerations, beyond those immediately suggested to us by an accurate and comprehensive survey of the facts themselves, on which our inference of the future fact is founded.—But to argue to the doctrine in the latter way, we must enter into abstract disquisition into the nature of virtue, and shew its necessary connexion with happiness—and, as it evidently does not attain that end in this life which properly belongs to it, we may then conclude, that there *must be* another state in which that end will be fully accom-

* Page 80, &c.

plished. Or, assuming the divine attributes as the ground of our argument, we may infer, that those who endeavour to conform themselves to the divine perfections, must, at some period or other, be rewarded by a God of infinite wisdom, goodness, and power, and, as the reward is not dispensed on this side of the grave, it must be reserved, in a state after death, for the holy and obedient. And, in like manner, we should draw opposite conclusions as to the ultimate end and recompense of vice.

Sometimes, indeed, we find an attempt made by writers to add to the evidence of a fact, by an appeal to the mode of its existence; and thus to exhibit an *analogical conclusion* as credible, from its agreement in the reason of it with the reason of the fact from which it is deduced:—as when Clarke introduces, after Origen*, a *probable account* of the resurrection

---

* The passage of Origen referred to by Clarke is the following: "Ἡμεῖς μὲν οὖν οὔ φαμὲν τὸ διαφθαρὲν σῶμα ἐπανέρχεσθαι εἰς τὴν ἐξ ἀρχῆς φύσιν, ὡς οὐδὲ τὸν διαφθαρέντα κόκκον τοῦ σίτου ἐπανέρχεσθαι εἰς τὸν κόκκον τοῦ σίτου· λέγομεν γὰρ ὥσπερ ἐπὶ τοῦ κόκκου τοῦ σίτου ἐγείρεται στάχυς, οὕτω λόγος τις ἔγκειται τῷ σώματι, ἀφ' οὗ

of the body into the illustration of it from nature, given in that passage of scripture, where

μὴ φθειρομένου ἐγείρεται τὸ σῶμα ἐν ἀφθαρσίᾳ. Contra Celsum, Lib. v. p. 246. Ed. Spenc.

Origen, it will be perceived, simply says, that a principle of preservation inheres in the body. Clarke however refines upon this explanation, observing, "It may also be supposed otherwise, *not without good probability*, that in like manner, as in every grain of corn there is contained a minute insensible seminal principle, which is itself the entire future blade and ear, and in due season, when all the rest of the grain is corrupted, evolves and unfolds itself visibly into that form; so our present mortal and corruptible body may be but the *exuviæ*, as it were, of some hidden, and at present insensible principle (possibly the present seat of the soul), which at the resurrection shall discover itself in its proper form." Clarke's Evidences of Natural and Revealed Religion, p. 206.

It is curious to observe, in this instance, the coincidence of argument between a defender of scripture indulging too freely in speculation, and a professed infidel. The objection of the infidel Paine—" that which thou sowest is not quickened except it die *not*"—is equivalent to this explanation of the fact of the resurrection advanced by Clarke: and it is strange therefore that Bishop Watson should have quoted this very passage from Clarke, expressing indeed at the same time his dissent from it, *in reply* to the absurd cavil of Paine. See Bishop Watson's Apology for the Bible, p. 360.

Saint Paul refers the sceptical inquirer concerning the resurrection of the dead, to the parallel instance of—the corruption of the seed sown, *preceding* its being quickened in the form of a plant. This is to weaken in reality the evidence obtained from the natural fact; as it is committed, in some measure, on the truth of the speculation associated with it; and the unsatisfactoriness of the explanation superadded excites a suspicion against the validity of the proper conclusion from the mere fact itself. The speculation here advanced, moreover, if just, would altogether destroy the illustration itself, with which it is conjoined; since the evident fact of—a decay, and a consequent restoration in nature—is what is required for the argument, in favour of the resurrection of the body, here employed: but, instead of our attention being fixed *exclusively* on this point, it is diverted, by an explanation obtruded on it, to the consideration of a supposed subsisting principle of preservation.—Still, we may discern a reason of a fact from which an analogical argument is deduced, and employ that reason in establishing the proof from the fact; so that the argument may involve, in the prosecution of it, both kinds of probability, and yet only indicate a likelihood in its result or application to the question in hand. Butler, for example, shews, by reasoning from the constitution of our nature, that virtuous habits are requisite to us, as finite beings endued with various propensities, in order to the perfection and security of our moral character; whilst he is pointing out the fact, as the ground of his argument, that the character of man is formed in the course of nature by the discipline of habits. Had Clarke, in like manner, brought some reason to shew, that a process of corruption might be a necessary stage, through which it is appointed that natural things should arrive at their perfect condition,—he would then only have confirmed his conclusion, by asserting the reasonableness of the fact on which his conclusion is founded.

But whilst both arguments may be brought into the service of Christianity, we proceed on much safer ground, when we appeal to real matter of fact, however inexplicable to us, in confirmation of its truth, than when we draw our proofs from the reason of the thing. In the first case, we produce our evidence for the truths on which we insist, and it is of that palpable kind that it cannot be rejected. In the latter case, we produce considerations founded on abstract principles, which are open to the denial of our opponents in argument. No one, for instance, whatever his speculative opinions may be, can deny that there are *signs* of a moral administration in the course of the world. But the advocate of the doctrine of necessity, or the philosopher who denies the fundamental existence of right and wrong as elementary principles to which all actions must be referred, is fortified against the conviction resulting from the notions of liberty and moral fitness.

It is not, however, to the more imperative nature of the argument drawn from the analogy of the natural world, but to its sober and cautious mode of proceeding, as distinguished from all speculations concerning the reasonableness of religious doctrines, that our observation must chiefly be directed, if we would remove from it the imputation of infringing upon the scriptural authority.

In forming an opinion concerning the reasonableness of any particular doctrine of religion, it is necessary to keep a constant check upon ourselves, lest we deviate into presumptuous speculation, and make theology the pastime, instead of its being the *discipline,* of the intellect. We have need to restrain the extravagances of curiosity by every barrier which a proper diffidence in our own conclusions can interpose. Here particularly applies that saying of Bacon:—" hominum intellectui non plumæ addendæ, sed plumbum potius et pondera; ut cohibeant omnem saltum et volatum ". How apt are we peremptorily to pronounce, that this or that doctrine of religion is inconsistent with Divine wisdom, or goodness, or with both, because we cannot reconcile it with our notions of those attributes, or make it appear to follow as a consequence of these notions; when perhaps, for aught we know, the doctrine so objected against, is an instance of the display of the very attribute to which it seems repugnant, and would appear strictly to follow from it, if we could only enlarge and correct our notion of it. Or even when we argue with the most pious intention of vindicating a doctrine of religion, as it is in the scriptures,—as in shewing the reasonableness of the doctrine of retribution;—may we not be too rashly concluding, that more is required to justify the providence of God, than God has willed to manifest of Himself; since what appears to us an *imperfect distribution* of rewards and punishments, may be nothing more than an *imperfect evidence* of the Divine attributes, suited to our present faculties and present condition of being? And how great is the danger, consequently, which we incur in the use of such an argument, of reducing the scripture-revelation to the fallible standard of human reason, and, whilst we impotently endeavour to make every thing in it appear reasonable, of enervating that authority on which our faith should implicitly repose?

But it is not so with regard to the argument from analogy. The form, indeed, of the argument is necessarily speculative, because, in order to apply our experience as a test of revealed truth, we are obliged to generalize our observations, and reason from them, as from general principles, to the particular facts which may be contained in an authentic revelation,—since it then follows, that, if such facts be contained in any given revelation, it may be said to exhibit a general identity of truth, as compared with the works of God: which identity is the bond of connexion, and proof of the identity of authorship, to the revelation in question, and the course of nature. But it is not speculative in its spirit and tendency*. By its very nature it

---

* " But if our philosophers have had little success in searching for recondite senses of scripture, their mistakes are more shameful and more dangerous, when they presume to judge of the divine economy; when they determine a revealed dispensation to be credible, or not, from preconceived notions of fitness and propriety, of justice and impartiality, which they boldly apply to the government of the Supreme Being. He cannot, they tell us, act in this manner; it would be contrary to his wisdom: nor in that; it would be inconsistent with his justice: one kind of degree of happiness he must be disposed to grant; another his creatures have a right to demand. But, whilst they throw out these peremptory assertions, not war-

represses curiosity, and silences the dogmatism of arrogant speculation. Instead of ministering to the pride of the human understanding, by proposing the doctrines of religion to the appro-

ranted by the observable course of God's moral government, nor by any known declarations of his will, they shew themselves to be unacquainted with the fundamental rule of their own science, and with the origin of all its late improvements. They argue like men who lived two centuries ago, inattentive to the difference between hypothesis and experiment. If, from a supposed character of the Deity, they undertake to derive his acts, and to trace the order of his Providence; however ingeniously the system may be formed, and by whatever demonstrations the several parts of it may be connected; yet the whole, having no foundation, but a precarious and arbitrary hypothesis, is easily overthrown. True philosophy would have taught them to proceed the other way: to begin with observing the present constitution of the world; with considering attentively, how God has made us, and in what circumstances placed us; and then to form a sure judgment, from what He has done, what it is agreeable to infinite wisdom, and the other divine perfections, that He should do. They might thus have learned the invisible things of God, from those which are clearly seen; the things which are not yet accomplished, from those which are." Powell's Discourses, Charge III. p. 342.

bation or disapprobation of reason—it humbles reason to an acknowledgment of them in their own mysterious character, by simply presenting their real, indubitable, counterparts in the book of nature. It sanctions no opinion relative to the invisible things of God, which is not warranted by real experience of the course of His visible administration. And if our opinions are only so warranted, it forbids us to question further. Whilst indeed we view opinions so formed, in juxta-position with corresponding declarations of scripture, we are effectually guarded against the imputation of a speculative theology. The correspondence itself in which the whole *effect* of our conclusions lies, is an answer to those who would accuse us as mere theorists in religion*.

---

* It is only in consequence of a like confirmation from an independent source, that the theory of gravity is justly not regarded in the light of *mere theory*. Thus Mr. Dugald Stewart has observed: " In this argument, as well as in numberless others which analogy suggests in favour of our future prospects, the evidence is precisely of the same sort with that which first encouraged Newton to extend his physical specula-

How sacredly the authority of the scriptures is preserved in the just prosecution of the argument from analogy, must appear to every attentive reader of Bishop Butler's admirable work. There is nothing which this great master of divine philosophy more condemns, than an intrusive spirit of speculation on religion from preconceived notions of the divine character. He continually insists upon the fact of our ignorance, by nature, of the ways of God, and the consequent necessity of our attending to those

tions beyond the limits of the earth. The sole difference is, that he had an opportunity of verifying the results of his conjectures by an appeal to sensible facts: but this accidental circumstance (although it certainly affords peculiar satisfaction and conviction to the astronomer's mind) does not affect the grounds on which the conjecture was *originally* formed, and only furnishes an experimental proof of the justness of the principles on which it proceeded. Were it not, however, for the palpable confirmation thus obtained of the theory of gravity, it would be difficult to vindicate against the charge of presumption, the mathematical accuracy with which the Newtonians pretend to compute the motions, distances, and magnitudes of worlds, apparently so far removed beyond the examination of our faculties." Elements of the Philosophy of the Human Mind, Vol. II. p. 422, 8vo.

means of information, which are spread before us, whether in the scriptures, or the book of nature. His is the true spirit of the philosophy of Bacon applied to theology. For he calls upon us to abandon our theories,—to curb our imaginations,—to lay aside our prejudices,—and to come, as athletes, bared for the conflict of severe inquiry into the truth, to the consideration of what the constitution of nature *in fact is*,—and accordingly to accept the conclusions to which such an inquiry may lead us, however repugnant to our antecedent views,—however unacceptable to speculative reason. Thus, he blames those who would form their estimate of religion, from conceiving the character of the Deity to be that of absolute benevolence: whereas the Divine Goodness, with which we are apt to "make very free in our speculations, may not be a bare single disposition to produce happiness, but a disposition to make only the good, the faithful, the honest man, happy " * :—and in the instance of

* Analogy, Part I. Chap. II. p. 47.

" It is to be considered that Providence in its economy regards the whole system of time and things together, so that

the doctrine of necessity, he points out the necessary existence of some fallacy in concluding against religion from that opinion,—shewing, by an appeal to the course of nature, that religion may be true, notwithstanding the opinion of necessity were true, and consequently demonstrating the *futility* of the opinion.—The practical object indeed of the whole work is, to inculcate on us the duty of receiving with *meekness* the engrafted word,—of girding ourselves with that sword of the Spirit, which alone is of temper

we cannot discover the beautiful connexions between incidents which lie widely separated in time; and by losing so many links of the chain, our reasonings become broken and imperfect. Thus, those parts of the moral world, which have not an absolute, may yet have a relative beauty, in respect of some other parts concealed from us, but open to His eye, before whom 'past', present, and 'to come', are set together in one point of view: and those events, the permission of which seems now to accuse His goodness, may in the consummation of things both magnify His goodness and exalt His wisdom. And this is enough to check our presumption, since it is in vain to apply our measures of regularity to matters, of which we know neither the antecedents nor the consequents, the beginning nor the end." Spectator, No. 237.

proof against the temptations, and difficulties, which beset the path of the religious inquirer; instead of vainly encumbering ourselves with the heavy armour of human reasonings. It pretends not to give a rationalized view of scriptural truths, though it proves unanswerably that the religion involved in the literal acceptance of those truths is a *reasonable service* *. The learning with which it would imbue the disciple of Christ, is that learned at the feet of Prophets, and Apostles, and Evangelists. The wisdom which it recommends and enforces, is that which has the fear of the Lord for its beginning—which soars aloft on the wings of prayer—and not that which unprofitably attempts to scale the heavens by steps of argumentation †.

---

* See particularly "The Analogy", Part II. Chap. VIII. the paragraph beginning with—" The design of this treatise is not to vindicate the character of God", &c. p. 389—393.

† How misplaced consequently is the sarcasm of Bolingbroke against this immortal work, as if it were to be classed amongst the reveries of speculative theologians!—" She, [the Queen,] studies with much application 'The Analogy of Revealed Religion to the Constitution and Course of Nature.' She understands the whole argument perfectly, and concludes

It deserves also to be noticed, with what scrupulous care Bishop Butler abstains from the introduction of discussion purely speculative into the argument of his work. The controversy respecting the identity of the divine attributes, as to their nature, with the human qualities of the same names, had arisen before the publication of his " Analogy "*: and yet we find an

with the right reverend author, that it is not 'so clear a case that there is nothing in revealed religion.' Such royal, such lucrative encouragement, must needs keep both metaphysics and the sublimest theology in credit"; &c. Bolingbroke's Philosophical Works, Vol. I. p. 123, 8vo, 1754.

* Bishop Butler presented his "Analogy" to the Queen in 1736. Archbishop King's "Sermon on Predestination", which was the occasion of the controversy here alluded to, was published in 1709. The question, however, had been first raised by Dr. Peter Browne, Bishop of Cork, in a Letter published by him in answer to Toland's " Christianity not Mysterious", about ten years before the Archbishop's sermon. But this Letter, being directed against the impugners of Christian mysteries, did not, it seems, awaken any controversy within the Church of England. It was the Archbishop's application of Bishop Browne's principles to the purpose of repressing the dogmatism of the Calvinist, together with some incautious statements which he had admitted in his argument, that

entire abstinence from it in the work. To have entered into it would have been to have deviated from the sound practical method of his treatise, into a speculation remote from the interests of human life. The outward operations of the Divine attributes, or their evident effects in nature, are the points about which his argument is concerned; and the conclusions which he deduces from these effects, are independent of any theory concerning the Divine attributes abstractedly considered. To have implicated, on the contrary, any abstract opinion concerning them with his induction of observed facts, would have been to have argued from abstract notions, and not *exclusively* from facts. Consistently with this adherence to matter of fact as the ground of his argument, he has detached the dissertations, on Personal Identity, and on the Nature of Virtue, from " The Analogy", in which they

brought the question prominently into discussion. Bishop Browne then resumed the subject in two treatises, which he successively published: " Procedure, &c. of Human Understanding", in 1729, 2d Ed.: and " Things Divine and Supernatural Conceived by Analogy, &c." in 1733.

had been originally inserted, and left them to be considered as independent discussions. So also he has avoided all inquiry into the immateriality of the soul, or into the nature of human liberty.

It cannot then be truly asserted that to attribute real weight to the evidence of analogy in accrediting our religion, exalts the authority of reason to a rivalry with that of the scriptures. Nay, the evidence itself compelling reason to be a learner in the school of nature, and to collect with patient and docile attention her faithful information,—how much more must it suggest to reason, the necessity of a devout submission to the authoritative word of the scriptures—those very instructors, to whose divine origination, and ampler fund of divine knowledge, it bears testimony?

Much, indeed, of that misconception which has arisen concerning what are called the distinct provinces of reason and faith, would have been avoided, had that fallacy been commonly guarded against, which is involved in the use of the word *reason*, to denote, at once, the *knowledge naturally* acquired by the mind, and the *faculties*, or *principles*, of the mind, by which it is acquired. We are apt, when we speak of any truth as a truth of reason, to impose on ourselves by a tacit belief, that it is a truth which is *taught* by reason. Whereas, in reality, " it is not reason, but experience which teaches us." The mere exercise of the faculties can teach us nothing. They may be employed indeed on themselves alone, and need no external objects, in such a case, as their material of instruction; but even then, it is from inward observation, or experience of themselves as distinct, in respect of their existence, from their mere exercise, that they *learn* the truths relative to themselves. A truth then becomes a truth of human reason, when the evidence of it is simply perceived by the mind; whose reason is thus informed, enlightened, and improved, as the recipient, and not the vehicle of knowledge. If we were always careful to preserve this distinction between our knowledge, and the faculties whereby we are made capable of it, we should not need to distinguish between the respective portions of our knowledge, by saying, that this truth belongs to reason, and that to faith. For it would then appear, that what we learn by supernatural revelation, and what we know naturally, are in the same sense truths of reason—truths, which reason accepts on the perception of their evidence.—Thus where Locke, contrasting reason and revelation, observes; " Reason is natural revelation, whereby the eternal Father of light and Fountain of all knowledge, communicates to mankind that portion of truth which he has laid within the reach of their natural faculties: revelation is natural reason enlarged by a new set of discoveries communicated by God immediately, which reason vouches the truth of, by the testimony and proofs it gives that they come from God,"* &c. —not to dwell on the looseness with which the terms *reason* and *revelation* are here employed †,—

---

* " Essay on Human Understanding", B. IV. Ch. xix. § 4. He proceeds to contrast them, as the eye and a telescope.

† There is a similar confusion in the following remarks of

it would have been more correct to have stated the same thing in substance thus; that nature

Hume. " Our most holy religion is founded on faith, not on reason . . . . " Of Miracles, Essays, Vol. II. p. 146.

" Divinity or theology, as it proves the existence of a Deity, and the immortality of souls, is composed partly of reasonings concerning particular, partly concerning general, facts. It has a foundation in reason, so far as it is supported by experience. But its best and most solid foundation is faith and divine revelation." Acad. or Scep. Philosophy, Vol. II. p. 183.

So also Clarke fallaciously contrasts reason and revelation, by representing that, to imagine them " at variance with each other, is the *like* absurdity, as supposing the eye to see contrary to what the ear hears, or that God should make one sense or faculty to contradict another." Clarke's Serm. on 1 Cor. i. 22, 23, 24. Works, folio, Vol. I. p. 501.

It must at the same time be admitted that it is the practice of the best theological writers to speak of reason and revelation, or reason and faith, as forming the two leading divisions of human knowledge,—understanding by reason all those truths which are obtained by the exercise of our natural faculties, and by revelation, or faith, all that is communicated to us by express message of God. It is not intended then, to object against such an employment of the terms, but merely to express a caution against the fallacy involved in an appropriation of them which use has established.

and the scripture-revelation were equally the appointed means of instruction from God, and that reason was the receiver and interpreter of both; the facts of both with their proper evidences being submitted to its assent,—and the assent consequently to a scriptural truth, however remote that truth may be from probability, being as reasonable, where the proper evidence of it is discerned, as an assent to the most common fact of experience *.

And here we may observe, the essential difference between the philosophy of Christianity and all other sciences. It is not to be sought *exclusively* in the system of the religion itself†,

* See Bishop Taylor's "Ductor Dubitantium", Book I. Ch. II. Rule 3. 20. Works, Vol. XI. p. 439—442.

† It is to such *exclusive* research into theological truth that the remark of the infidel, stigmatizing theology as a *false science*, justly applies. "La superstition dominante épaississoit les ténèbres. Avec des sophismes, et de la subtilité, elle fondoit cette *fausse science, qu'on appelle théologie*, dont elle occupoit les hommes aux dépens des vraies connoissances." Raynal. "Histoire Philosophique et Politique," &c. Tome I. p. 9.

but in a comprehensive view of both dispensations of God—the natural and the scriptural—taken together as correlative parts of one great system of divine instruction. Philosophy, then, when applied to religion, consists in the accurate generalization of particular instances of theological truth communicated to us by an authentic express revelation from God; so as to exhibit them in their points of coincidence with the facts of nature. It is, on the other hand, the reduction of facts of the same kind to some single principle, which constitutes the business of all merely human philosophy. The logician, for example, is occupied, in developing the theory of reasoning, shewing how all particular arguments are reducible to the principle of the syllogism: the natural philosopher, in explaining the phenomena of motion by the law of gravitation: the moral philosopher, in asserting some theory of our moral sentiments, referring them either to the principle of conscience, or prudence, or propriety, or sympathy, &c.

We may not, indeed, be able in many departments of nature, to arrive at any single principle, so as to solve by it all the phenomena in them. All motion may not proceed from one physical cause. The principle of magnetism may be essentially different from that of gravity. Still it may be maintained, that the effort of the mind is to devise some one comprehensive theory by which all phenomena of one kind may be united; and that, where it fails in obtaining such a theory, it loses the *full* satisfaction of philosophy. It only acquiesces in any result short of this, as an approximation to the point which it desires to reach. The pursuit of such a result appears to be necessarily implied in those two fundamental rules of philosophy; " that not more causes of natural things be admitted than are both true, and suffice for the explication of their phenomena": and, " that of natural effects of the same kind, the same causes be assigned as far as is possible."

The philosophy which the labourers in the field of human science pursue is, accordingly, an investigation of ultimate principles,—they endeavour, not only to trace connecting principles among the events of nature, but to simplify to the utmost the discerned connexions between physical events. But in divine philosophy we must repress this endeavour after simplification. We must be content to hold all the truths which are the subjects of it, as ultimate principles. For we know nothing of them beyond themselves, as a collection of attested facts presented simultaneously to our contemplation. We have no knowledge of them as antecedents and consequences, as we have of the facts of nature; and therefore, as our only mode of judging of the existence of necessary connexion fails us in regard to them, we have no reason to suppose, that any one truth of scripture is the grand antecedent of the rest, or the master principle by which the whole congeries of scripture-truths may be combined. Indeed, the absurdity of attempting so to combine them, is demonstrated by the erroneous views of Christian doctrine to which every such attempt invariably leads. For instance, if we assume the divine predestination as the great principle of our theological system, we expose ourselves to the absurdity of denying that God has bestowed the gift of a perfect free-will on man;—and we destroy the moral force of God's promises set forth in scripture,—and the efficacy of prayer;—and, in short, we disparage the whole revelation of Christianity, by subordinating it to an abstruse metaphysical tenet*:—if we assume the Divine benevolence as our principle, we perplex ourselves with difficulties concerning the punishments actually inflicted on men in this world, or threatened in scripture:—if, again, we assume the sanctifying grace of the Holy Spirit as the principle, we impugn that law of Providence which assigns reward and punishment to every man according to his works, and weaken the ascription of our salvation to the atoning efficacy of the Redeemer's blood†:—if, lastly, we as-

---

* It is not strange therefore, that Calvin should have been called upon to defend himself against a charge of Arianism, and that his doctrines should have been suspected of an Unitarian tendency. See Dr. Miller's "Observations on the Doctrines of Christianity in Reference to Arianism," p. 131, 150.

† Wesley carried his notion of the practical holiness implied in sanctification so far, as even to profess " to regard the atonement of Christ, as at length necessary only for procuring

sume, as our ultimate principle to which every other doctrine must bend, the doctrine of justification by the merits of Christ, we incur the danger of Antinomianism; and we impair, in our exclusive zeal for the honour of God the Son, the integrity of the doctrine of the Trinity; overlooking the *equal importance* of the relations which we bear also to God the Father, and God the Holy Ghost*. These instances

pardon of erroneous opinion occasioning erroneous practice; the true believer becoming, in process of time, incapable of committing any more grievous offences." Id. p. 142.

The doctrine of imputed righteousness has a similar tendency. Here we may observe a theory of the mode in which the benefit of the atonement operates, introduced to the destruction, not only of other doctrines of scripture, but even of that doctrine upon which it attempts to refine—for, the righteousness of Christ being supposed transferred to man, the necessity of a *continued* reliance upon the atonement made for sin is superseded.

* Is not this, practically, the effect of discourses from the pulpit which are confined to a reiteration of the doctrine of the atonement, to the exclusion of the coordinate topics in the scheme of Christianity? A belief in the Trinity may be conscientiously professed; but at the same time, if the believer, in the cultivation of his religious principles, is taught to look

may well convince us, that,—however to superior intelligences the aggregate of religious doctrines may appear true, from their agreement with some one ultimate principle equally pervading them all,—*we* can only *know* them as *individual* facts connected with each other in one scheme; or as instances, for the most part, of *different principles* of Divine Providence, which it belongs not to us to reconcile with each other, whilst they must be held by us in perfect concord*.

to the Second Person alone of the Trinity, he is led to act as if the *whole* doctrine were not true.

* And yet, in creeds or articles of religion, certain points may be selected as necessary to be believed, without disparagement of the integrity of scripture: for here the question is, what things are necessary to be confessed in order to church communion; it being impossible, from the nature of the case, to comprise every point in such formularies. See Stillingfleet's Works, Vol. IV. p. 51. folio; Powell's Discourses, Charge I. p. 301; Balguy's Discourses and Charges, Disc. VIII. Vol. I. p. 113.

The Articles of the Church of England not consisting so much of affirmations of scripture truth, as of negations of doctrines unscripturally introduced into the body of the faith; it is evident, that their whole drift is, to maintain the *exclusive* au-

If the integrity of scriptural truth had been thus scrupulously respected by all expositors of Christian doctrine; what a legion of phantom doctrines, which the spells of an unhallowed ingenuity have called into being, would have been hushed in silence, and remained unknown in the nothingness from which they came?—If every distinct intimation of scripture had been held as a distinct principle of theological truth; and—however it may have been combined with other

thority of scripture, and not to limit it by selection. Upon the same principle of excluding heretical opinions as they arose, may be accounted for, the greater length of the two later creeds compared with that called the Apostles' Creed. And, though in the Athanasian it is said, concerning the believer, that "before all things it is necessary that he hold the Catholic faith"—which faith it explains to consist in a right notion of the Trinity,—we ought not to suppose that it states one doctrine as necessary above all others; or that certain niceties of discrimination in our view of a particular doctrine, are essential criteria of a saving faith;—but that the doctrine of a Trinity in Unity, when disencumbered of its unscriptural additions—as including all others, or as a comprehensive expression of all scripture-truth—is necessarily confessed in the true confession of Christianity.

truths with which it coalesced, yet, where it did not so coalesce,—had been regarded, as admitting of no compromise or diminution, in order to reduce it to greater conformity, but as demanding to be retained in all its repulsive inconformity; there would then have been no occasion for the invention of hypotheses, to reduce into an arbitrary order the various declarations of the sacred volume:—but Christians would have *implicitly* followed its dictates; and, in forming their system of belief, would have invariably enlarged their theory, so as to embrace all the facts developed in scripture, instead of curtailing the facts to the limits of their theory. We should not have found some drawing distinctions between doctrines, as necessary and less necessary, or as speculative and practical, and thus charging with superfluity the riches of the oracles of God: but whilst, in a systematic arrangement of the truths revealed, some were assigned to the foundation of the building, and others to the superstructure, they would have been careful to exhibit the *whole edifice* of religion, as it stands in its fair proportions in the scriptures themselves; as scrupulously maintaining the necessity and importance of the *superstructure* as of the *foundation.*

The inquiry, which it was purposed to make, has now been prosecuted in its several parts. The grounds on which the philosophical truth of Christianity may be established, have been explored and shewn to be valid. For it has been pointed out, that there must be certain principles, or laws of the Divine administration, common to the revelation of God contained in his works, and that delivered by any authentic messengers of his word.—The necessary existence of such common principles has been argued, from the impossibility of communicating to man, as he is, even by an express revelation, any knowledge of God *essentially* different from that acquired by experience; and from the necessary relation which all revealed truth has to human conduct.—The nature of the credibility derived to a supernatural revelation, from its coincidence with nature in these common principles of the Divine administration, was then shewn to be, that resulting from the evidence of analogy:—since, both, from the form in which the truth expressly revealed is conveyed, and from the object to which it is peculiarly directed, as contradistinguished from our natural knowledge, it must differ from the latter, in the degree in which it evidences these principles; and since, analogy is the mode of reasoning which enables us to estimate an essential agreement in truth, under the different modifications of it produced by difference of circumstances. —And, as it is essential to a just analogy, that the difference between the truths which it connects, should be only such as may be conceived to result from the difference of circumstances respected in each,—it was further shewn, by some examples, that the doctrines of Christianity may be regarded as identified with those modifications of theological truth, which result from a reference of the general principles inferred from experience, to the circumstances of the invisible world; or, in other words, are the true analogies to the course and constitution of nature.—Hence it followed, that particular doctrines of Christianity are proved by this Evidence to be, *like* known facts, or approximations to the truth; though not actually *verified* to their full extent, yet to be rendered credible, as found in the volume of revelation; whilst, at the same time, from the confirmation thus obtained to the theory of the religion, even such doctrines as do not appear to have any counterparts in the system of nature, participate in the light of the Evidence.

From the consideration of the nature of the credibility obtained from the Evidence to the doctrines of scripture, we passed on to survey its importance under the several points of view which it presents: first, as a speculative argument to the truth of a revelation; secondly, as a practical proof; and thirdly, as a ground of illustration.

As a speculative argument—it was shewn to be demonstratively conclusive only, as a test for trying the falsehood of a pretended revelation; but, in the case of Christianity, to be of peculiar weight, as an answer to a challenge on the part of the religion itself, and consequently a proof of a coincidence of *design*, in the structure of the religion, and the constitution of nature ; and, that though it suggested no direct answer to particular objections against Christian doctrines, it removed them entirely as arguments against the truth of Christianity.

As a practical proof—the Evidence in question has been pointed out, as demonstrative of the expediency, practicability, and immediate personal interest, of the religion which it accredits :—since it exhibits the principles of the religion in actual operation ; and connects what we are called upon to do, as believers, with our business in familiar life.

As a ground of illustration—its value in opening the mind to the reception of mysteries, and in removing vague prejudices, has been deduced; first, from the nature of analogy in general ; and then, from the peculiar force of analogies connecting the things invisible with the things of the visible world ; and from that important relation which this kind of evidence, on the whole, bears to the essential miraculous testimony—as counterpoising the natural improbability of a revelation by the proof of internal probability.

Lastly, such objections as appeared to militate with the preceding observations, and to throw suspicion over the application of the Evidence, have been considered, and, it is hoped, have been satisfactorily refuted:—and, at the same time, the refutation of such objections has afforded an occasion for distinguishing the Evidence obtained to Christianity by this method of inquiry into its credibility, from arguments tending to establish the reasonableness of the religion; and for assigning to the philosophy of Christianity its appropriate character.

But, after all that has been urged, the real worth of the Evidence remains to be appreciated by each person in his own convictions, from an actual application of it. It is an evidence, whose force cannot be fully argued out and placed before the view. It must be felt, in order to be rightly understood. For, it is the testimony of the spirit of natural piety pleading the cause of the great Author, at once of nature, and of the inspired word, to the heart of man. By those, who would be acquainted with a series of beautiful applications of it, and probe its logical accuracy, The Analogy of Bishop Butler must be diligently revolved :—but still, to obtain that animated sense of the truth of our religion which this Evidence is capable of affording, each person must explore it in the observations of his own experience, and listen to its dictates in the "still small voice" of conscience. At the same time let it not be supposed, that it appeals ultimately to the arbitration of so capricious and fluctuating a thing as mere inward sensation, which may, or may not, be real and natural :—the appeal which it makes, (and which is a sound and immutable criterion of religious truth,) is to authentic principles of our nature, as they have been implanted in us by the Creator. A conclusion drawn from the perfect congruity of any truth with these principles of our nature, —with those of the heart as well as those of the intellect,—(for our whole nature implies nothing less than this ;)—though the process by which we arrive at it be imperceptible to us, and be incapable of being stated in words, is as sound a logical deduction as one that is formally obtained from stated premises *. If, then, these inward principles start as it were into life, and thrill with the delight of kindred association, on the perception of religious truths,—there is the strongest testimony in these genuine emotions, that the religious truths which awaken them, are the words of Him who knows what is in man †,—that the message, which thus fills us with all joy and peace in believing it—lifting up our hearts and understanding to God—forcing us to "confess Him without confession", and to adore Him without adoration,—must be indeed the voice of glad tidings,—the sounds of " glory to God in the highest, on earth peace, good-will towards men." For these principles of our nature stand as the last beacons, ap-

---

* One of the alternatives of the dilemma proposed by our Lord to the Jews concerning the baptism of John, was an appeal of this kind :—" But if we shall say, of men; we fear the people : for all hold John as a prophet."

† See Mr. Miller's Bampton Lectures, Lec. 4, 5, and 6.

pointed to bear the immediate intelligence of a true religion to the mind of man. Miracles, and prophecies, and all the various arguments drawn from collateral considerations, are but so many successive luminous points of transmission. But when these kindle up with brightness, they point to the unbroken line through which the sacred light has been propagated, and proclaim its authentic derivation from the Father of Lights himself.

If, now, so powerful an evidence to the truth of our religion is couched under the circumstances of the world in which we live, it is not only against scriptural truth that the infidel is found to harden his heart, but against the clear admonitions of the voice of Nature. As our Lord told the Jews, that, if they " had believed Moses, they would have believed Him, for Moses wrote of Him";—so may it be said to the infidel, that, if he believes the instructions concerning God which are contained in the natural world, he ought to believe the truth of that supernatural revelation of God, to whose authenticity the natural world gives its suffrage. Otherwise, his only consistent refuge is in mere speculative theism, or rather in atheism. For he must deny the voice of Nature, to be the voice of God, if he would evade the inference necessarily resulting from such an admission; and thus impugn that very doctrine of final causes, upon which the proof of the existence of God mainly rests. Since—if he asserts that a design to instruct cannot be argued from the evident effects of such a design—there is no greater reason in any *other* instance, that design should be argued from its effects: and thus the principal ground for supposing an intelligent Author of the universe would be altogether removed. The only argument consequently that would remain to him, would be that drawn from metaphysical considerations, which, taken alone, must by their nature be insufficient to any real practical belief in a God. God must be discerned as the actual governor of the universe, to excite in us the sentiments of hope, and fear, and love towards Him:—and what is a professed belief in Him without these sentiments?

Indeed, the more strongly that any one advocates the excellence of the light of nature, the more irresistibly is he led by his own concession to the lamp of God shining in the scriptures. For, to him, to whom the light of nature shines most vividly, the ways of God in the world, as far as they are made known by that light, must appear most conspicuously, unobscured by those mists of error through which the less informed intellect surveys them. And the person, accordingly, who really feels the strength of uninspired reason in searching the deep things of religion, must be excellently disposed by nature, for receiving that illumination from heaven, which finds its chief obstruction in the prejudices of our earthly imaginations.

The firm believer in Christianity may also obtain a needful discipline to his mind, in cultivating an acquaintance with the philosophical evidence of his religion. It is not sufficiently attended to, in general, that our conviction of the truth of our religion is an improvable talent—improvable, not by the simple accumulation of evidence only, but by the exercise and strengthening of those principles of our nature, by which the evidence is appreciated. From that corruption, which has spread its canker to the very vitals of our reason, we are, naturally, slow to believe, and incompetent to judge fairly of the pretensions of a divine revelation. But this slowness and incompetence may be overcome by effort on our part; and the task of thus preparing the way of the Lord, is no inconsiderable part of our religious trial. It may not be in our power, at any particular period, to estimate the full force of the evidence with which religion proposes itself to our belief; but it is always in our power to cultivate, or neglect, those habits of the mind which tend to form the right disposition for religious inquiry. And the degree of satisfaction, which we may attain in the inquiry, will depend on the pains that we have bestowed, and are continuing to bestow, in disciplining ourselves beforehand—in clearing away the prejudices of the understanding, and purifying the heart.—Now, in the process of collecting evidence from the course of nature, we are continually bringing into exercise those moral and intellectual principles, whose healthful energy is involved in the act of faith. All other evidences lead the mind to God only in their result. We are busied chiefly, either in arguing from human sentiments to the character which must belong to the oracles of inspiration, or in estimating the weight of human testimony; that we may ultimately infer a superhuman origin to the religion of the scriptures. But here, it is not only the result of the examination which carries the mind to God, but, in the process itself, we are immediately concerned about the signatures of divine agency impressed on nature, and approaching the Revealer of religion at every step which we advance. We are engaged in separating the things of the world from their mere temporary uses, and referring them to their grand and enduring purpose,—that purpose which will continue to be accomplished, when they shall have passed away themselves, and time shall be no more,—the glory of the Almighty Creator and Governor. We are thus cooperating with the effect of religion, and are predisposing ourselves for the reception of its influence.

Dull and insensible must be that heart, which does not feel itself softened and improved by contemplations of this kind,—which does not burn within, whilst it hears the Author of nature thus graciously talking with it by the way, and expounding to it the scriptures. The perception of the evidence demands no constitutional fervour,—no extraordinary power of mental abstraction,—no solemn sequestration of the thoughts and affections from the business of social life,—no experience in the ecstasies of fanatical empiricism. It presupposes only a candid temper of mind—" intellectum abrasum et æquum"—that simplicity which our Saviour enjoins where he says, " if thine eye be single, thy whole body shall be full of light"—which he illustrates to us by the example of children, and commends in the person of the guileless Nathanaél,—and which is mentioned as a characteristic of the first Christian converts under the expression of " singleness of heart." They who apply themselves with such a disposition to a contemplation of the ways of Providence, have brought their minds to that state, in which they correspond, at once, with the order of external nature, and the invisible economy of grace; and readily interpret, therefore, what they see without them, or hear of God, by what they are in themselves. In such persons, the word of the Lord, whether written "in the volume of the Book", or indicated by signs in the visible world, will have free course, and be glorified. As they enlarge their observations, by unwearied habitual study of both oracles of divine instruction, their increase in holiness and piety will be coincident with their increase in knowledge—their minds will be more and more conformed to the Divine image—and, to their purer view, apparent anomalies in the course of the Divine proceeding, will be gradually resolved into instances of that scheme of providence with which they once seemed irreconcileable. Thus going on from strength to strength, in cooperating with that Spirit, which is the efficient cause of all that is good, and wise, and powerful in man, through His gracious influence, the believer may aspire to that height in the sublime philosophy of Christianity, which is a demonstration of its truth, more divine than that resulting from mere argumentative discussions; where " perfect love casteth out fear"; where the disciple becomes the saint; and the docility of the child of grace is consummated in the mature experience, and the wisdom, of the man of God.

THE END.

G. Woodfall, Printer, Angel Court, Skinner Street, London.

www.ingramcontent.com/pod-product-compliance
Lightning Source LLC
Chambersburg PA
CBHW081215170426
43198CB00017B/2623